Leadership, My Way!

Coming Full Circle

Marian White-Hood

ISBN 979-8-89243-263-4 (paperback)
ISBN 979-8-89243-264-1 (digital)

Christian Faith Publishing
832 Park Avenue
Meadville, PA 16335
www.christianfaithpublishing.com

Printed in the United States of America

If you have a strong purpose in life, you don't have to be pushed. Your passion will drive you there.

—Roy T. Bennett, *The Light in the Heart*

YOUR THOUGHTS?

CONTENTS

PREFACE

Like many people with a degree in education, I began my career as a teacher in a suburban school district. Although I was assigned to a high school, I did not know what teaching was all about. As an African American woman, I did not know what I did not know.

My first teaching experience was in a high school. It was horrendous, frightening, and downright disturbing. My first year, I was placed on probation and treated like a second-class citizen. The devil's favorite words are *give up*! I did not feel what I was supposed to feel for the craft of teaching until I was transferred to a middle school in the same district.

There, I fell in love with a group of struggling pre and early adolescents. I understood and adopted the terms *diversity* and *inclusion*, *teamwork*, *cooperative learning*, and *groupthink* before they became buzz words. I wanted to support the students who were from various backgrounds, cultures, and lifestyles; protect them; listen to them; connect with them; and love them.

I immersed myself in the space called middle school. I remained at this school for thirteen years, and during that time, I learned from six different principals. Two of them taught me what not to do. I was able to become the teacher that my students deserved. In fact, these principals helped me truly connect with the education profession.

My story is *not* remarkable, but it is compelling. It is unembellished and sometimes austere! This story is about living out values and convictions, making mistakes, and rebounding as God intended, becoming a vessel driven by the human experience. In the early 1990s, God was doing miraculous things in my life, restoring me, empowering me. I was able to move forward and was better for it... leading, my way.

INTRODUCTION

Potential—Who Can I Be?

Like many African American students graduating from high school in the late 1960s, I was told by my counselor that I would not be able to go to college because I was not good enough. Brokenhearted, I cried many tears and was confused, troubled, perplexed. I always made *good* grades! I was considered the *wallflower* of the neighborhood—always staying in the house after school, always doing my homework, always reading. Everyone called me the bookworm!

Something was terribly wrong. I did not realize it until later, but no one ever prepared me for college. No one taught me how to study. In fact, my high school did not build a bridge for students like me to navigate college well.

My mom wanted to help me but only had a sixth-grade education. As a single parent, working three jobs, she was unable to attend PTA meetings and open-house programs. I secretly wondered if she was afraid to meet my teachers, afraid that she would be disrespected or belittled or even dehumanized because of what she didn't know—how to help her daughter. I worried because Mom just had a sixth-grade education. Would she be intimidated by administrators and teachers?

I prayed with my mom who was determined to help her daughter succeed. Mom saved enough money to pay for the application fee. So I applied to Howard University in Washington, DC, and was accepted. There were preconceived opinions and personal biases concerning college admission for Black students. But for me, college admission was not just wishful thinking. I wanted to attend a college…so bad that it hurt deep in my soul. I yearned for a college education. I don't even remember why or how or who put that notion… that dream…that yearning in my head.

My first semester was difficult, and I was placed on academic probation. I prayed and studied, prayed and studied. I began to undergird my study with more prayer. I knew that trusting the Word of God was essential. I knew that God was my doorkeeper—he could open doors. So I promised myself that I would do my best to excel at Howard University.

By the second semester, I was receiving As and Bs…off probation. I was on the road to pursuing my passion of becoming a college graduate. A degree would determine my life chances.

As I studied and studied and completed each course, I wondered, *What if?* What if my professors were poor teachers? What if I did not understand the terminology, concepts, and theories? What if my profession did not care about me? What if the professors were like the teachers that I had in high school? Those who dehumanized me daily? What if the professor cared more about writing and publishing, conducting research to advance his or her own career than mentoring or coaching a student who needed help? What if my professors spent little or no time supervising students like me, served on too many academic and administrative committees, and never reached out to his or her students? What if?

Well, I studied all day and late into the night. I was able to get a part-time job in the summer. To save money, I walked to the college—almost five to six miles depending upon the shortcuts through the city, walked through the alleys and through parks. I prayed, cried, and then prayed.

My mom taught me to show *grace* or the strength God sends us so I could live like a true Christian. She told me to let go of the *hard feelings* that I had about high school teachers and college professors. My mom told me that the strongest person is the one whose soul is clean for God and others. "Take it to the Lord in prayer"—her favorite words. I began to understand and *love* the Word. It changed me. I was able to bag up those hard feelings and replace them with feelings of hope, faith, and forgiveness.

By my third year of college, my grades and attendance were strong. I was strong! I was able to select a major. I knew that I would begin a journey in education. I was thirsty for the journey. I was drawn to the road less traveled…I wanted to travel through the theories, through history, through the forest that would lead to a career in education. This journey would help me live my best life as an educator.

An Aspiring Teacher's Journey

When it was time for me to declare a major, I thought about my high school experience, including teachers who yelled at me and degraded me. I didn't remember their names. But I remembered begging, *helpless* and unprepared. The following are some of my memories:

- My teachers did not make a real effort to help me learn.
- I felt in my heart that the geometry teacher did not have patience with me, and I cried every night. He taught me to *hate* math. One day, my mom went to the school to meet with my geometry teacher and share her concerns. But the teacher did not display empathy or concern. When Mom came home, we cried together.
- My mom and I prayed over the situation—I was depressed.
- My counselor told me that I was not good enough for college.
- I didn't know my principal's name.
- This poor little Black girl was a wallflower. Yet I had dreams of becoming somebody.

What I *did* know is that I wanted to help students engage in lifelong learning, prepare for careers and the world of work, meet the challenges of global citizenship…be better than I had been at eighteen years old.

I believed that teachers needed to be able to walk in the shoes of their students. They needed to reflect on their practices—evaluate what was working and what was not. They needed to step outside of themselves to understand and truly help each student succeed. I wanted to become a teacher!

The Journey Begins: Becoming a Teacher

The times: in 1970, teachers in the District of Columbia threatened to strike. The reasons were the same then as they are now—low salaries and poor benefits, testing, lack of support including resources, teacher shortages, and student discipline or attendance problems. But somehow, for some reason, I was drawn to teaching. I guess you could say that God lit the path. I knew that I had to walk it.

After graduation from college, I applied for a teaching position in a local school district. Although I needed a couple of classes for certification. I was hired and given a chance to teach in a high school. That opportunity helped me grow. I had unprecedented challenges, unprecedented opportunities!

I was assigned to a school and was the only Black woman in the department. I did not have a classroom—I was a "floater." I had no supplies, no handbook, no support, and I did not know how to navigate the school. Within a few months, the principal called me in his office and informed me that I was on probation. I think word about it got around the school. It seemed that everyone in the school knew about my situation. Once again, I felt demoralized. I felt like an idiot; I felt stupid! The principal made me feel that way.

I remember a Caucasian teacher who drove me to the bus stop one day. As we drove past the principal and administrators who were on bus duty, my friend screamed out, "Get down! Get down!" I quickly obeyed her. Later, I learned that she did not want to be seen with me. I was dehumanized again! After two years, I was transferred to a middle school and flourished as a teacher for the next thirteen years.

What Good Teaching Should Look Like

I taught home economics and love it! I learned that my students needed to be exposed to activities that helped them to learn:

- How to manage themselves
- How to manage relationships
- How to make responsible decisions
- How to become self-reflective
- How to develop positive student-teacher relationships
- How to be trustworthy and dependable
- How to set goals and plan for the future
- How to prepare for life beyond the classroom and much more…

However, in middle school, I was indoctrinated (like many educators) to believe that teaching was about increasing academic achievement test scores and preparing students for the world of work. But the good thing is that I was a home economics teacher, able to plan with academic teachers. Interdisciplinary planning, they called it. I loved it and learned a lot from academic colleagues.

Teachers were represented by a union and pushed for increased pay and resources. I transferred to a junior high school. They talked about "working to the rule." I was opposed to this primarily because I did not understand it. Why would anyone want to deny students after-school support? As a home economics teacher, I arrived early—at least one hour before school opened. I stayed late to work on projects, bulletin boards, lesson plans, etc. How could I join the teachers? *No!*—"working to the rule" would not work for me.

Unfortunately, I was bullied by several teachers and my principal. Someone placed rotten eggs in my mailbox. Someone flattened my tires. I received negative notes and ugly stares from some teachers. I went to the principal to voice my concerns and seek help.

He stated, "That's what happens when you don't side with your union. I can't help you."

Those words resonated with me for weeks. They haunted me. I was not a happy, excited, enthusiastic teacher any more. Instead, I lost my edge and feared some of the teachers. I was intimidated by what was becoming a hostile environment.

One day, during my planning period, I sat at my desk and began to cry. This would have been impossible but for a fortuitous circumstance. To my surprise, I received a visit from a parent who happened to be a supervisor in the school system. She introduced herself and shared that her daughter told her that her Ms. White, her favorite teacher, was hurting. That's when I learned that a teacher's body language and demeanor communicate volumes to students. The supervisor listened and encouraged me to be strong.

Almost immediately, I noticed a change in the principal's attitude. During a faculty meeting, he communicated that negative behavior by teachers creates a toxic culture for students. "This will not be tolerated," he stated.

The next year, we received a new principal. Things changed! I continued to work in the school and loved it! What had been a plain, sometimes unclean, and ordinary school became a place where teaching and learning was expected and welcomed. I noticed that the teachers changed. And the students were thirsty for engagement!

During my thirteen years as a teacher, I began to question myself. Again, I asked myself the question, "What if?" over and over. What if I tried harder? What if I visited students' homes? What if I used my salary to purchase the materials the students needed? What if I bonded with the students to learn what they really wanted and needed?

I met a young man and became engaged to be married. I decided to invite my students to be part of the ceremony. Thirteen girls were my bridesmaids and six boys to be ushers. I purchased the material, patterns, and supplies for all my students.

The classroom was full of excitement, and the children worked so hard to complete their garments. The boys made their own ties and vests in the home economics class; the girls made their long gowns as part of a class project. Needless to say, the sleeves on dresses were lopsided; hems were uneven; the vests were too short; and the boys' ties were different sizes and widths. The entire staff came to the wedding including the principal.

Once again, I returned to the road less traveled to seek another degree. I went to the university in the evening and taught school during the day. I used my summers to reflect on my practices. In fact, each summer, I began to write about my experiences and lessons learned.

As I wrote in "A Phenomenological Platform for Teaching At-Risk Students," in *Illinois Teacher of Home Economics*, v33 n3, January–February 1990, 101–102, I believe that teaching at-risk middle school students was the phenomenological platform, a powerful theme for becoming. The process involved exploring real-life situations, considering community and world problems and solutions, and translating this into action. I was able to blend theory with practice. Soon, I became an award-winning teacher.

My Philosophy as a *Developing* Teacher

I believe that students can become all that they can be in an ideal learning environment. I believe that the classroom should be neat, attractive, and child-centered. I believe that every student needs the support and guidance of a teacher who is positive, nurturing, and caring. I believe that an effective teacher will create lesson plans and activities that motivate, intrigue, and inspire his or her learners.

I aim to grow as a teacher with my students. I believe that there will be difficult times, challenging times, and times to cry, but I will not be afraid of the tasks ahead. It's a journey…a lifelong commitment to grow together, not a short trip. We as teachers can't dillydally, dawdle, or crawl. We must view teaching as an excursion, a trek, a mission.

My tool belt included the following:

- Student-centered practices
- Nurturing, warm, and supportive approach
- Social skills
- Choices and opportunities
- Conflict resolution
- Strategies to build relationships with students
- Focus on the whole child
- Goal-setting and planning
- Helping students reach their goals
- Classroom discussions or dialogues and conversations
- Academic press, coaching and mentoring
- Confidence-building
- Showcasing student talent
- Good attendance—being present

I remember a pastor saying, "Break the power of the past by living for the future." By my third year at the school, I knew that I wanted to be a part of something larger than my classroom, myself!

I wanted to spend more time with my students. At the home economics department meeting, I learned about a student organization called Future Homemakers of America (FHA). I began doing research and soon learned how to get my students involved in the group. FHA aimed at preparing today's students to be tomorrow's leaders in the home and workplace. On June 11, 2020, the organization celebrated its seventy-fifth anniversary and legacy of making a difference in families, careers, and communities across America.

I fell deeply in love with the organization, it's goals and mission. I loved its mission, goals, purposes, and the opportunities that it provided youth regardless of race or gender.

Goals and Mission of Future Homemakers of America

Goals

1. To provide opportunities for personal development and preparation for adult life
2. To strengthen the function of the family as a unit of society
3. To encourage democracy through cooperative action in the home and community
4. To encourage individual and group involvement in helping achieve global cooperation and harmony
5. To promote greater understanding between youth and adults
6. To provide opportunities for making decisions and for assuming responsibilities
7. To prepare for multiple roles of men and women in today's society
8. To promote family and consumer sciences and related occupations

Mission

To promote personal growth and leadership development through family and consumer sciences education. Focusing on the multiple roles of family member, wage earner, and community leader, members develop skills for life through character development, creative and critical thinking, interpersonal communication, practical knowledge, and vocational preparation.

Creed

We are the Future Homemakers of America. We face the future with warm courage and high hope. For we have the clear consciousness of seeking old and precious values. For we are the builders of homes, Homes for America's future, Homes where living will be the expression of everything that is good and fair, Homes where truth and love and security and faith will be realities, not dreams. We are the Future Homemakers of America. We face the future with warm courage and high hope.

I introduced the club to my students, and *we*, together, became a local chapter with awesome student officers and energetic members.

Later, several of my officers became state officers…later national officers. In fact, I had three national officers over the thirteen years. I was elected chairwoman of the National Board of Future Homemakers of America. My principal and superintendent approved of my travel to different states, conducting trainings and chaperoning my officers, who also conducted trainings for their peers and attended national conferences with me.

It was surreal, something that I would never have dreamed of. Eventually, it was a big deal for my state and national officers, the state of Maryland, my school, and myself.

Like the song lyrics, "Yesterday, all my troubles seemed so far away." All my feelings, emotions, and do-overs were faraway yet helped me become a new person, a national leader for an organization that I believed in. I was the first African American chairwoman! The organization's mission and values became my north star. I became a model for my students and the best version of myself.

I learned so much from the students, who were actually learning from me. Words like *social justice, community action, family engagement*, and *human relationships* were integrated into many of our focus groups and conversations.

However, we were driven by the word *leadership*. It meant so much to us; in fact, we used the term at least ten times a day—working after-school, planning schoolwide activities, working in the community. Our club became an integrated part of the classroom. The good thing is that classroom leaders emerged throughout the year.

Someone once said, "If you want to serve, you must be a servant." Thus, the leadership style of most of the class leaders was democratic and participatory. We delved deep into emerging issues, brainstormed solutions, and formed plans to address the issues as students and members of our student organization. The students grew emotionally, socially, intellectually, and creatively. Instead of exclusionary, we were inclusive. Everyone—regardless of race, ethnicity, gender, or background—was a vital individual in the classroom. We realized that everyone had a special gift. To whom much is given, much is expected.

Leadership, Their Way! The Gifts State Officers Gave Us

Kim—fourteen years old, a model of friendship and teamwork, self-discipline, patience, values, health and wellness, family focus

Cheryl—fourteen years old, a model for social justice, interpersonal relationships, ethical action, family

Latonya—fourteen years old, a Black female, a role model of character and professional demeanor and an excellent communicator.

In 1989, I became an assistant principal. In 1993, I was summoned to the superintendent's office and asked if I wanted to be a principal.

I hesitated…and then said, "But I love teaching! I love my school. I love working with students."

He said, "You were an outstanding teacher, and outstanding teachers make great principals."

I was reluctant because I did not think that I was worthy enough, didn't know enough. And the what if's began to consume me.

I thought of one of my sheroes—Marva Collins. I thought about my past and what I could bring to the table as a principal. Then I thought about *me*—an *African American* female principal who struggled personally and professionally. But negative self-talk was counteracted by the superintendent's positive remarks. I think you know where I'm going with this. I was honored to be in his presence!

I was blushing to hear what he had to say, "You are a competent educator. You are ready for the principalship."

Then I responded, "Yes, I truly want to be a principal!"

The Making of a Principal

I learned a lot from six former principals—what to do and what not to do. I recalled their words—words that made me stronger.

My Six Principals

Principal 1—Always stay positive. "It's a great day inside and outside the school."

Principal 2—"I have a vision for this school."

Principal 3—"I want you to join our team. We are going to a middle school conference to learn about the middle school concept."

Principal 4—"I can't make a decision without teacher input."

Principal 5—"We can make it happen!"

Principal 6—"That's a great idea! Let's do it!"

One of the six principals provided opportunities for teachers to attend conferences; the provided educational articles for teachers and time for teachers to connect with one another as part of their planning time. He provided teachers with great mentors. Side bar: I had three mentors. He also seemed to love being a principal and often said that being a principal was his life—"the best job in the world."

Another principal said that the principalship allowed him to touch more lives. He seemed to be in every classroom. It was like building his own house, selecting teachers and creating a learning community. He seemed to know every student's name and invested time in activities that students and parents enjoyed. He was highly visible.

Still another principal was known for his fairness and ability to listen to teachers, parents, and students. He worked to promote school spirit.

One principal was a mover and a shaker. He delved into curriculum, provided us with resources, and professional development opportunities. He was talented at developing leaders in the school—from department chairs to team leaders.

I believe that all these principals were honest. In fact, I was mesmerized by each principal, so I took notes and learned from each one.

I wanted to spend time with students in the school, ensure that students had a positive school environment by sharing my passion, values, and philosophy of education. I wanted to make a meaningful impact as an educator in the community. I wanted to examine all the feelings and memories of my past to make a better present and future for the students in my care.

I wanted to blend all the great educational theories with my personal practices. I wanted to be intricately involved with the dynamic of school and the drama of the learner.

During my early years as a leader, I met someone who taught me how to think…think in different ways. At the University of Maryland, I met Dr. Francine Hultgren and began to explore the human perspective. Each course, each article, and every presentation drew me nearer, closer, deeper. Her brilliance is found in the following resources:

- Lashley, M. E., M. T. Neal, E. T. Slunt, L. M. Berman, and F. H. Hultgren. 1994. *Being Called to Care*. Albany, New York: State University of New York Press.

- Berman, L. M., F. H. Hultgren, D. Lee, M. S. Rivkin, and J. A. Roderick. 1991. *Toward Curriculum for Being: Voices of Educators.* Albany, New York: State University of New York Press.
- Hultgren, F. H. 1995. "The Phenomenology of 'Doing' Phenomenology: The Experience of Teaching and Learning Together." *Human Studies: A Journal for Philosophy and the Social Sciences* 18: 371–388.

There are personal and private stories that cannot be shared—ups and downs, scratches and scars, wounds that healed and some that will never heal. Stories of people who nursed me through it all.

I could share how my truth was exposed; how I dug deep into the text of my life, reflecting on my transformation and what it meant to me. I could share my rites of passage.

Dr. Hultgren was the thread that ran through it all, the mentor who caused me to face the realization of what I could be.

As a doctoral student, I studied how to understand the meaning of the "lived experience" under Dr. Hultgren. My qualitative research included exploring the lived experiences of pre- and early adolescent females in middle school. I was able to question and examine their world. Through this research, I was able to engage in critical thinking while plowing through mountains of texts—the dialogue and conversations with participants in the study. I analyzed data and discovered compelling truths that stand the test of time. These truths ground my actions even today.

Commentary

xxv

CHAPTER 1

Becoming a Principal

The reoccurring question: What would give my life more meaning?

How could I counter the narratives in my educational background? Those comments made by my high school teachers, negative counseling, pervasive headlines and articles about the crisis in education were becoming a hardship. How could I counteract the stuff that made me cringe years ago?

I enrolled in the University of Maryland to pursue a doctorate. It was the best of times and the worst of times. I am blessed to have grown as a teacher and gained a unique understanding of pre- and early adolescents through an ethnographic study that I conducted while in the classroom. My study took me through hermeneutics and interpretation, critical theory, and the world of middle schooler.

I observed six principals along the way. Was that enough to integrate what I learned in college with what I observed about my principals and administrators? What would I do differently? There were no sounding boards for me. Who or what would guide me? How? When? And what does that guidance look like?

My Truth, My Being

I enjoyed providing age-appropriate experiences for students, preparing students for college and careers including vocational education, serving families, coaching and mentoring teachers, using data to drive instruction, writing curriculum, teaching all levels and ages, engaging parents, and organizing and planning programs.

I worked in the educational field for many years. I loved my life as a teacher. Yet I believed that there was something more that I should be doing. I wanted to do the heavy lifting. I soon learned that heavy lifting cannot be done alone.

I believed that I was a lifelong leader, a professional developer, a passionate child advocate, educator, relationship-builder, and an experienced problem-solver.

Why Did I Want to Become a Principal?

I enrolled in the district's training program. Everyone said, "Make a difference." I applied for a principal's position and was finally summoned to the superintendent's office.

He stated, "If you can inspire students...if you can inspire teachers, you can reach children. I wanted to reach beyond my class-room to touch more young lives. This was my truth!"

On the way home from the meeting, I thought, *You have to be a qualified teacher to become a principal.* I had been an award-winning teacher, team leader, department chair, and assistant principal. I repeated, "Yes, I can. Yes, I can. Yes, I can do this!"

Principal White-Hood

I wanted to ensure that all students had an *amazing place called school*—a place where they could learn and prepare for global citizenship. I wanted students to be a part of something that I never had in the 1960s—a real school.

I was appointed to middle school in August 1993—hmmm, not much time to learn the lay of the land! I replaced a principal who was well-known and respected. I actually shadowed her when I was an assistant principal and learned a lot. I was grateful that Dr.

——— was an excellent principal who completed many tasks such as scheduling, hiring, room assignments, and much more. The school received the United States Department of Education's Blue Ribbon Schools Award. She was an outstanding principal who knew how to get things done.

So I knew that I had big shoes to fill in a few weeks. My process:

- *Pray, pray, pray*
- Meet with the administrative team members
- Meet individually with teacher leaders (department chair, team leaders, etc.)
- Meet with the PTA president and other officers
- Begin communicating with the community
- Meet with several parents representing the various teams
- Meet with several students from each team

I began to think about my strengths and challenges. I met with the math department chair to review the state testing data and met with the English chair to analyze the reading data. I realized that even though reading scores were increasing, math scores were dismal. Over the weekend, I locked myself in my office and tried to envision how I wanted the school to look and be like for our students.

Think-Abouts

How I Was Treated as a New Teacher

I wanted to be part of the solution.

I loved working with parents and their families.

I wanted to help more students go to college.

I was unafraid of bigness, of handling challenging situations

I wanted to change the narrative!

I remembered a course in grad school—Curriculum, Instruction, and Assessment (CIA)

I wanted to ensure quality instruction for all.

I was inspired, empowered, and wanted to collaborate with teachers to ensure quality instruction—how could *we* do this together?

What would have the best impact on the school?

My vision for the school was clear!

I wanted our middle school to be epic! Legendary!

I was willing to do anything, willing to outwork my doubts and fears! But how?

I crafted my philosophy (drawing from pieces of the past). I recalled examples of teamwork, parent engagement, etc. Then I focused on a theme for the school under my leadership: *aim for the top...because the bottom is overcrowded!* The theme reflected the person I imagined myself to be.

Making Memories and Becoming the Principal I Wanted to Be

Each day, I arrived to school at 3:00 a.m. and often stayed late. I loved to be in this school because it felt like a learning place—clean, colorful, warm, and inviting.

I wanted to ensure that students have a positive school experience. I wanted them to have positive teachers, dedicated role models, and thought-provoking quotes painted on the walls in the cafeteria, halls, locker rooms. I wanted administrators who would believe in the collaboration and the TEAM concept—you know, *together, everyone achieves more*. I wanted to be the principal who used the triangle approach:

1. home
2. school
3. community

Defeat was not an option! Children would always be at the center of the triangle. I wanted to be described as follows:

Personal and Professional Attributes

caring	tolerant	positive	professional
trustworthy	adaptable	self-aware	dependable
supportive	creative	inspirational	respectful
selfless	empathetic	strategy	humanistic
transparent	energetic	honest	patient

What Was Different?

Our administrators planned bus tours around the community that we served the first week of teacher training. All teachers in the school had collegial mentors. In fact, we began mentoring clubs and activities for girls and boys as well.

The "Aim for 100 Mentors Day" was a huge success and helped us identify numerous mentors who were recruited to support the reading programs, homework or projects, and a variety of events (field trips, competitions, fairs, etc.) In addition, I provided opportunities for teachers to attend professional conferences and trainings.

I prayed with my mom every night; prayed for teachers, mentors, and volunteers: and prayed for parents. I sponsored administrators, lead teachers, and aspiring administrators who traveled to conferences, participated in timely trainings, and visited other schools to observe and grow. Naturally, we created new teacher symposiums and biweekly mentor focus groups. There were countless opportunities to provide our students with successful role models, career exposure.

I met with my leadership team to review data each week. Issues emerged that haunted me. Many of our eighth-grade students seemed complacent—they didn't have career goals. I met with counselors regularly and learned that our students needed more exposure. They needed to see and learn more about other communities, counties, states, and regions. They needed to *be there*, *be present* to explore possibilities.

When asked to develop goals and vision statements, many of the students struggled. To tackle this issue, I asked the counselors to help plan local college visitations during October College Week. Every day of the week, eighth-grade classes visited colleges and universities locally—for example, Bowie State, Howard University, Towson, Coppin State, University of the District of Columbia, American University, Georgetown University, Goucher College, Catholic University, Trinity University, and many more made the list. Each year, the program was expanded overnight, over the weekend, three-day trips, etc. We toured colleges in North Carolina, Pennsylvania, Florida.

We turned college week into college month and, later, creating a college-going culture. We included daily PSAT vocabulary for seventh and eighth graders, PSAT seminars for eighth graders, and administration of the PSAT to eighth graders.

There were times when we struggled as a school—when three students died; when great teachers were promoted and we had to rebuild teams; when our enrollment sored and we received sixteen temps and new teachers in August (just one month before school was to open). Negative voices will always play the loudest!

My administrative team had superpowers! They were able to counteract the negatives. I will never forget those incredible people! Instead of the half-empty glass, each team member asked, "What's possible? Where do we go from here?"

Outstanding Educators—the Leadership Team

Ms. Melissa—Full of ideas, talented, creative, and a joy to be around; the young teacher who became a team leader, later an administrator; and now serves as an award-winning principal in a nearby school district.

Ms. Cheryl—A beautiful soul! This talented teacher was a mathematics and technology genius, loyal, kind, and student-centered.

Ms. Ellen—A talented home economist who later became the magnet coordinator. She stood by my side every day and never gave up on me or the students.

Ms. Francis—Not only was she wise but extremely knowledgeable about *everything*! She was the English Department chair! We traveled to Germany together, training principals and helping them create mentoring programs in their school.

Ms. Mark—A powerful young math teacher who became a team leader. He was a confidant, pillar of strength, and a leader that all students respected.

Mr. Bittinger—Known for his creative scheduling! This counselor was sought-after by other principals in the district every year because of his expertise, but he stayed with us. His projections were spot on. From 800–1,600 students and 16 temporary cottages, this counselor (and department chair) was able to make it work.

Ms. Shirley—A beautiful role model and an amazing counselor who was promoted.

We planned the work and worked the plan. We were in it together! Each member of the team knew that he or she would be tasked to on-board new staff in the department; become a collegial partner; support and coach others; to actively listen; help staff navigate the middle-school way; communicate and share information; listen, connect, learn, and grow; and ensure clarity. So what did their leadership mean to our teachers and students?

Know that our administrative team made a restorative impact! Can you imagine a world without them?

Just what did their leadership look like?

- relationship-builders?
- fact-finders?
- mission-driven?
- balancing home, church, school, community?
- all of the above?

Their leadership looked like the following:

- Professionalism
- *Growth and development—all levels*
- Everyone is learning…everything (but not always at the same time)
- Partnering and networking
- Changing posture
- Modeling
- Continuous improvement
- Flexibility
- A vision that includes the whole child
- Excitement, energy
- Contingency planning
- Preparing
- Mentoring teachers, parents, and staff
- Everyone involved in school improvement
- Training—being aspiring leaders

- High-quality learning environment for all students and families
- Being accountable!

As the word *accountable* exploded on the middle-school scene, it took on different meanings. It impacted my principalship, the leadership experience.

What was behind accountability? What was the driver?

- Fairness, integrity, honest, ethical, morally responsible
- Inclusion, equity, parity, and diversity
- Empathy and tolerance
- Trustworthiness
- Attention to detail
- Checks and balances
- Fear
- Diplomacy
- Truth
- Answerability
- Obligation
- Loyalty
- Communication
- What's right!
- Leadership
- Framework for evaluating progress

Just What Does It Mean to Be a Principal?

Grace! I recall a situation with an art teacher. For some reason, we were at odds with each other, and our unions were involved. The battle was on! But in reality, we were fighting the same war. We both were fighting for educational excellence. One day, the teacher visited my office; we looked at each other and began to cry. *Grace!* We both knew that *forgiveness* opens doors. Ms. ——— and I became great friends, respecting each other's point of view and working together to build a strong art department. I think the experience of forgiveness laid a strong foundation for my leadership journey.

There are many issues to face, many variables to examine. During the years of my middle-school principalship, I learned that the principalship was political. I learned that social justice was embedded in the role of the principal. It became apparent that *grace* was a huge part of my being.

I also learned that there was no treatment for the do-nothing disease or mediocrity. If I did nothing, who or what would I become?

I'm reminded of the incident concerning a male teacher and a female student at—— MS. It occurred on school property, the last day of school in June. After the incident, I became despondent, a recluse! I found myself isolated from friends and family. For two weeks I was in a fetal position, in bed. I was deeply concerned for the girl and overwhelmed that evil entered one of our classrooms—my school. Even though the incident occurred after-school hours; it was on school property. This incident let me know that a principal's presence is 24-7.

Several staff members criticized my lack of support for the teacher. But our speech pathologist met with me, and I knew that God sent her to revive me. I did the right thing! I grew from the incident. One need not be afraid of stating facts, of speaking up for justice, of telling the truth.

Yes, sometimes things seemed pretty *dark*. Our God will fight for us. I was amazed at the pouring of support I had from the community, political leaders, parents, the press, and the clear majority of the teachers. Being a principal means humbling yourself and cherishing the moments when you look to God for answers, and you do the right thing.

I began to appreciate the teachings of Dr. Asa Hilliard, *Recognizing an Institutional Racism.*

I became infatuated with our district's Black male achievement initiative. This fueled my soul, and I turned to the following resources for comfort:

1. Comer, James P. and Alvin F. Poussaint. *Raising Black Children: Two Leading Psychiatrists Confront the Educational, Social, and Emotional Problems Facing Black Children.*
2. James P. Comer is the author of ten books, including *Maggie's American Dream* and *Leave No Child Behind* and the recipient of many honors and awards, including forty-seven honorary degrees.
3. Lezotte—In 1991, Lezotte published *Correlates of Effective Schools: The First and Second Generation*, describing the seven correlates of effective schools:
   - Instructional leadership
   - Clear and focused mission
   - Safe and orderly environment
   - Climate of high expectations
   - Frequent monitoring of student progress
   - Positive homeschool relations
   - Opportunity to learn and student time on task
4. Hammond, Darling. *The Right to Learn, Teaching as the Learning Profession, Preparing Teachers for a Changing World.*

Every now and then, I pull these resources off my bookshelf and flipped through the dog-ear pages, reading the highlighted passes.

I realized that my desires were the same as most beginning principals. I wanted to do many things:

1. Form long-lasting relationships that is inspiring, engaging, and involving
2. Be visible
3. Actively listen
4. Think outside the box—test the limits so to speak
5. Be transparent and authentic
6. Share a sense of purpose

7. Mentor others—help others become leader
8. Lead the instructional program
9. Build teams
10. Reflect on one's practices
11. Observe, interpret, and analyze
12. Humble self
13. Reverse the order of things
14. Be the model
15. Do what you want teachers to do
16. Communicate, communicate, communicate
17. Be witty—use humor
18. Lead everything related to teaching and pedagogy

Someone once said, "The principalship is the best job in the world."

I wanted to be a mirror. The principal can see an exact reflection of who he or she really is. We need to *stay close to the students*; never forget what it means to be a teacher by teaching a class, demonstrating a strategy or method, substituting. We must continue to interact with students. We must be present for the staff, parents, and students. We must codify the best practices (visiting other counties and states to learn best practices). We must serve on committees to help shape policy; recruit, select, train, and retain teachers. Remember, we must focus on your purpose. You will reach your destiny.

I had a mentor who reminded me frequently that "What we do here changes lives everywhere!" So what should we do? Who should lead the way? What are the components of the vision for this school?

Vision for Middle-School Improvement

- Conduct needs assessments
- Engage the team in decision-making
- Provide professional development
- Create a college-going community

- Build out career coaching processes and targets
- Develop strategies for alumni and mentor engagement
- Create and nurture a community to address school challenges
- Provide a wide array of appropriate resources on careers exploration, internships, and colleges
- Design case management and tracking strategies
- Build student's self-confidence and *grit*
- Create bridging programs (sixth to seventh, seventh to eighth, eighth to ninth grade)
- Plan and articulate with elementary, high school, and college
- Expand counseling opportunities—drop-in programs
- Research feasibilities
- Conduct crosswalks
- Recruit and train the brightest staff members
- Ensure cross-cultural communication
- Design high-quality professional development
- Promote a laser-sharp analysis of data
- Use data
- *Ask* and continue questioning: What about implementation? What about monitoring practices?

I thought over and over, *Don't the students deserve to see what's outside the neighborhood, community, county, state? Shouldn't we expand what is…look at what can be done for them? And if God gives you leadership ability, use it wisely!*

Research continues to suggest that students need out-of-class activities that promote social development, academic performance, expanded worldview, cultural diversity, social responsibility, career or college exposure, and increase self-efficacy or esteem. So I provided an expanded activity program.

An Expanded Inclusive Activity Program Model

- college field trips
- PSATs in grade 8
- Rose Court
- gentlemen's club
- summer bridge
- Saturday camp
- winter-break camp
- gospel choir
- computer club
- sports and athletics
- band and orchestra
- content area clubs
- art club
- STEM
- culinary
- dance and aerobics
- drama club
- debate team
- comic book club
- AV club
- Sunday dream keepers
- Spanish club
- yearbook club
- literary club
- National Honor Society
- peer tutors
- conflict management team
- science bowl
- spelling bee club
- math league
- community service club
- student council

- National Junior Honor Society
- Future Teachers of America
- Odyssey of the Mind
- mock trial club
- mentors club
- prayer club
- Future Business Leaders of America
- entrepreneurship club

I realized that I needed to think out of the district's box. Ideas jumped from my head—ideas about the following:

- curriculum and instruction
- guidance and counseling
- alternatives to suspension
- experiential learning
- interdisciplinary instruction
- personalized learning
- our bench strength—creating aspiring leaders' program
- creating an academic ambience

I shared my thoughts with my leadership team. They joined me visiting schools in other counties to get ideas from the school lunchroom program (software) to the student organizers (agenda books); from curriculum to instructional delivery. We absorbed everything that was tangible, relatable, and evidence-driven.

We went in as researchers with no preconceived notions. We prepared general questions; we did our homework, reviewed school data posted on the MSDE website. During each visit, more granular questions emerged. We met with student representatives to obtain their perspectives and lead teachers to seek and understand their viewpoints.

One thing was clear, we wanted to ensure an authentic relationship with our students...identify usable strategies to promote interacting with students and parents; parents in the evening and on weekends.

I was on fire, aroused by the inspirational messages of James Comer, Lezotte, Alvin Poussaint, Linda Darling-Hammond, and John Murphy. Reading and studying their research, findings, philosophy, and recommendations was an opportunity for growth and development. I attended national conferences (NASSP, NAESP, ASCD, and others), local and state meetings, enrolled in courses, and surrounded myself with smart, smart, smart people. I hoped that some of their brightness would rub off on me.

<hr>

White-Hood's Sayings

- "Listening ears," allowing you to hear concerns
- "Eagle eyes" to observe students being good
- "An enthusiastic voice" for announcements and cafeteria duty
- "A kind heart" to nurture students, parents, and staff
- "Direct integrity"
- "Never demeaning but demanding"
- "There is no *I* in *team*.
- "You cannot spell *success* without *u*."
- "I had more skills and talents than I knew I had."
- "Great principals are great teachers. They know what good teaching looks like and what good teaching feels like."
- "Grow and go!"
- "What would you be able to write if the *E* key was broken? The *E* key is important for thousands of words in the English language. If you are the *E* key and you are broken, what would we be able to do?"
- "White-Hoodisms: give respect, get respect. Everyone is a learner. You are unique. You are queens and kings. You are strong. I expect great things. I care about you, etc."
- "Recognize…"

By 1998, our student numbers increased to 1,600 with over 90 staff members in the facility built for 800 students. We had 16 temporary buildings that we lovingly called cottages. We had 4–5 security staff members, affectionately called the A-Team.

Our data points revealed that we would need to double down on our academic program strategies including tutoring, homework, help, Saturday bridge programs, counseling programs, and interventions, mentoring and coaching, extracurricular incentives, recognition programs. One thing I learned: you can't let people tell you that you can't do something that you feel is innovative because it's just never been done before. So I held deep-dive sessions to dissect the mathematics and English and reading curriculum. For example, I remember working at Children's Hospital during college. The doctors and nurses created a Kardex for each patient that included medications, activities, medical needs and services. I shared the information with the administrative team, and we decided to create a Kardex for all our underserviced children. Each Kardex captured educational services, instructional materials, reading and mathematics challenges and strategies, resources and projects that each student would complete with the support of teachers.

Then we ramped up our testing intervention strategies. The second quarter was challenging. I read somewhere that the second quarter grades are often disappointing as middle school student interact more with their friends and less with their homework. Once again, I looked "up and out" focusing on my Lord and not myself. I knew that he, and *he* alone could resensitize my consciousness, helping me focus on what is possible.

Sometime in the spring, I received a phone call from the county executive office informing me that a busload of legislators was scheduled to tour our building. The group included members from the Board of Education. Little did I know that this was like a feasibility-study group. The goal was to determine if there was a need for a second middle school in the area.

When the group boarded the bus for departure, I was told that one member stated, "This is a security nightmare."

Later, I learned that a new middle school would be built approximately one mile from our middle school.

My seven years at the middle school penetrated my soul in the most dynamic and forceful ways. There was love, respect, energy, growth, and achievement. CIA—curriculum, instruction, and assessments—were strong. Our motto was *Aim for the top…because the bottom is overcrowded.* I was going through a unique transformation. Everything about me changed—my attire, my walk, my dialogue, my relationships, my outreach. I was truly on fire, and I cried tears of joy.

My professional mentor advised me to start writing about my journey. So I began to write at least one theme-focused article every summer—a mental release and a part of my journey.

Leadership—What It Meant to Me in 1993

Thoughts on Leadership

Leadership is not about titles, positions, or flowcharts.
It is about one life influencing another.
—John Maxwell

Management is doing things right; leadership
is doing the right things.
—Peter Drucker, *Essential Drucker*

Great leaders can see the greatness in others when
they can't see it themselves and lead them to their
highest potential they don't even know.
—Roy T. Bennett, *The Light in the Heart*

Leadership is about making others better as a result of your
presence, and making sure that impact lasts in your absence.
—Sheryl Sandberg

A leader…is like a shepherd. He stays behind the flock, letting the most nimble go out ahead, whereupon the others follow, not realizing that all along they are being directed from behind.
—Nelson Mandela, *Long Walk to Freedom*

Great leaders create more leaders. Good leaders have vision and inspire others to help them turn vision into reality. Great leaders create more leaders, not followers. Great leaders have vision, share vision, and inspire others to create their own.
—Roy T. Bennett, *The Light in the Heart*

Leadership is lifting a person's vision to high sights, the raising of a person's performance to a higher standard, the building of a personality beyond its normal limitations.
—Peter Drucker

It's okay to admit what you don't know. It's okay to ask for help. And it's more than okay to listen to the people you lead; in fact, it's essential.
—Mary Barra

Leadership should be more participative than directive, more enabling than performing.
—Mary D. Poole

You may encounter many defeats, but you must not be defeated. In fact, it may be necessary to encounter the defeats, so you can know who you are, what you can rise from, how you can still come out of it.
—Maya Angelou

White-Hoods Standard of Care for Youth

First, do no harm.
Ethics and care.
Attention to inclusion and diversity.
Cultural relevance.
Address needs, interests, strengths, and weaknesses of the whole child.
Community of care and support for students
Use every opportunity to do something good for others.
Serve where the need is.

The Principal's Rose Court

One day, I was in my office and an eighth-grade girl came to see me. She was crying and said that she didn't want to go to class anymore. She said that she was not learning anything new. However, she had an A average and yet sullen. So we talked for about thirty minutes, and then I walked her back to class.

For two weeks, girls visited my office, saying they were bored. They piled in like beautiful flowers, and most of them sat on the floor around my desk. It was like circle time in preschool. Soon, there were twelve girls, and I called them my dozen roses. They gathered in my room at lunchtime and sometimes after school. I posed questions—for example, What do you want to talk about? Why? What do you like to do after school? What are your favorite classes? Why? Tell me about the class. And, then I would ask them to explain themselves. What is your evidence? Why did you think that?

I started to get phone calls from parents, thanking me, asking if my group was a real club. The school became an honor's club for girls. Over the summer, I received numerous calls from parents asking if their girls could join the "principal's club" in September. Wow! How would I handle this request?

I began to think, reflect, and even *pray*! The answer(s) emerged brilliantly. I called the group Rose Court. We would meet one evening each week; sometimes on Saturdays for a special field trip or activity; sometimes before school at 6:30 a.m.

I shared a draft of the program with several female teachers who were extremely popular and well-loved by the students. In the hands of the teachers, the program blossomed! The male teachers began to inquire about the group and asked if they could start one for the boys. The male club was called the Gentleman's Association.

This journey was life-changing…being a principal yet teaching and mentoring students! I felt called to do more than "principal" a school. I was mesmerized by my own life—being close with the students and leading a school. On my way to work, I would listen to "Morning Mood" by Edvard Grieg—instrumental music. It was a time to be thankful, reflect, commune with nature. This caterpillar was becoming a butterfly.

Major Components of the Rose Court and Gentlemen's Club

- adult mentors
- parent involvement
- parent leadership
- cotillion for girls and beautillion for boys
- field trips
- spa days
- focus groups—topical issues
- organizational structures (officers)
- program of work
- student portfolios
- monthly themes
- careers, college awareness, social skills,
- recognition or celebrations
- sister circle or brother circle
- lock-ins for read-a-thons

Focus Areas

- academics (quarterly progress reports)
- family, friends, and special people
- fundraising
- physical fitness
- grooming
- health and nutrition
- communication and speech
- college-going culture

What Touched Me

- Number 1—Over the years, I attended four student funerals—one male and three females. The death of my students was traumatic. Two girls had adolescent cancer; one girl was a diabetic; and a boy died of an allergic reaction in ninth grade. I visited hospitals often. I founded myself drained, but I knew that I had to allow myself to feel.
- Number 2—The music teachers recruited children for a gospel choir. It seemed as though all the children in the school wanted to join. And the choir was spectacular. I envied every student because I could not carry a tune myself. I found myself crying at the school concerts… could not contain myself. "Eyes on the Sparrow" was one of my favorite hymns. My passion for music caused me to hire more music teachers, purchase more instruments, and provide time in the schedule for students to practice.
- Number 3—I received a phone call from the superintendent inquiring about the Rose Court. He indicated that a parent in another school complained to him that there was no group for the boys. Little did she know, but the Gentlemen's Association was in full force, and the advisers were male teachers who gave up their time to develop the

program for the boys. I was protective when it came to the clubs because I knew how important they were to the students.

- Number 4—I wanted every middle school student to have a mentor and to be involved in a club or learning organization. Research suggested that students who were actively engaged in group sports, music, teams like debate team and math teams, and special events were more likely to excel in something that interested them. Thus, the leadership team designed monthly and evening activities like the spelling bees, *Family Feud* games, *It's Academic*, field trips to Johns Hopkins Hospital, and *Jeopardy*. I combed the community and the district for mentors and coaches because I knew that our middle school students needed positive role models and experiences. I promoted a variety of activities because I did not have these activities when I was a teenager. I felt in my heart of hearts that *access* was vital to our children. No door should be closed. I fought for access and opportunities.

- Number 5—The data provided evidence that *active engagement* worked. Each month, we celebrated students of the month; each quarter, we celebrated the members of the 3.0 and 4.0 clubs; each year, we sponsored an academic banquet for students and their families. We knew the names and interests of all the students. We met weekly, monthly, and quarterly to review the data points for students (i.e., suspension, references, test scores, attendance, grades in each subject). The department chairs met with their teachers to collaborate on strategies and examine classroom data with a magnifying glass—a laser-sharp analysis of standards, domains, and targets using data such as test scores, quizzes, and exit tickets. In addition, the chairs worked with the administration to identify ways to help teachers who we considered to be our best weapons against student failure. We held Saturday school, winter-break school, summer school, and after-school tutoring, and homework support. I found ways to fund the programs. It became a passion, and I became more assertive in my quest.

- Number 6—I focused on data, day in and day out. I provided opportunities for our lead teachers to have time in the schedule to share data and use it. Our data management system produced positive results. We celebrated the students, teachers, and parents. We *boldly* traveled where no one else had been that year from the bottom of the district data charts…climbing up and onward.

- Number 7—When our school district was busy dealing with bomb threats during the state-testing window, I decided to spend the week in the school. I locked myself in every evening. Purpose: to ensure that no one entered the building unlawfully. Every morning, I would get up, take a shower, and get dressed. I stood by the doors of the school greeting the teachers and assuring them that *no one* entered the building with dangerous materials (i.e., bomb materials). In addition, several of our parents were policemen. They brought bomb-sniffing dogs to the school to check random lockers each morning. Thus, we were able to test our students without interruption. Some principals thought I was *crazy*! But in reality, I was *bold*! I wanted to protect the school; I wanted the feeling tones to be correct, nurturing, and peaceful.

- Number 8—And then there was *9-11*! A dark worldview covered the school, district, state, and nation. I began to think that people were shedding their values, giving in to fear. What would the world become? I prayed for peace, tranquility, safety, and security. I prayed for my students, teachers, and parents. I prayed for my mom, brother, family, and friends. I knew that we would never be the same. I humbled myself and leaned on the Lord.

The Lord is my rock, my fortress, and my deliverer; my God is my rock, in whom I take

refuge, my shield and the horn of my salvation,
my stronghold. (Psalm 18:2)

He heals the brokenhearted and binds up
their wounds. (Psalm 147:3)

- Number 9—My sister passed away while I was a principal. She was a loving person who devoted her life to nursing others. I increased the frequency of my physicals (at least twice each year) and tried to become a vegetarian. This worked for about five years. Then I returned to doughnuts and coffee every morning, fast foods for dinner, and ice cream for my nighttime snack. Later in life, this regimen caught up with me.
- Number 10—Here's the good news about the police. Short story! I was on my way to school and bumped a *stop* sign. Of course, I was pulled over by an officer who immediately asked for my identification. I pulled my license from my purse. The officer said, "Oh, you're Dr. White-Hood! No worries. Consider this a warning. Be careful and slow down." I smiled and thanked him. I was assertive – Proud to be a well-known principal of the school, proud to be a member of the community, proud to be supported by councilmen.

My Truth

As a new principal, I worked with my school community to develop a plan to promote a college-going culture. We uncovered barriers to success and sought resources to address them. As a middle school principal, I worked with my team to form special programs for students most at-risk and ramped up efforts to support all students.

Yet I was outgrowing my school by leaps and bounds. I was limited by my walls, the ceilings, and the role of middle school principal. I didn't want to become an existential threat.

So I sought a position that would blend my educational practice with higher education and research. I was excited and believed that I would be a tremendous asset to my next assignment. I loved what I had become. I was ready to dream big.

Lessons Learned

The most time-consuming and energy-draining task of implementing the system can make or break the leader. When trying to address systemic challenges, don't confuse boldness with arrogance, assertiveness with aggression. The effort to do the right thing is always well worth it.

Commentary

CHAPTER 2

Preparing to Be Founding Principal

I received a phone call asking me to report to the area superintendent's office. I was nervous beyond words. But I trusted him. My evidence? Many times, I had to visit his office, I found the area superintendent reading Hebrews 11:1, "Faith is the assurance of things hoped for and the conviction of things unseen."

When I arrived, I was pleasantly surprised! The area superintendent informed me that I would become the founding principal of a new middle school. He shared some information with me and thanked me for my efforts at my first middle school. He also commended me on some articles that I wrote and honors that I achieved. This conversation was designed to build me up…help me arrive at a decision—to take on another leadership role or to stay at my current school. The new school was to be a technology magnet school. As principal, I would be able to select my staff, galvanize parents to form focus groups to work on a name change, theme, colors, mascot, etc. I would be released from my current school to begin planning with district leaders—the design of the building, offices, classrooms, furnishings, technology, curriculum, etc. What an enormous honor!

This was a time to celebrate! That evening, I tossed the worst-case scenario around in my head over and over. The *what ifs* emerged. I drew from my grounding…the spiritual enrichments and edification that anchored me. I prayed with my mom almost every night. I accepted the new assignment that summer I moved out of my middle school to an empty space in another school, began the enrollment process, and recruited teachers and administrators. My car became my command center. I visited neighborhoods, feeder schools, and other principals. I attended community meetings and shared my struggles with the Lord. "We walk by faith not by sight" became my theme song!

Dreams do come true! I envisioned the new school as "a true learning organization." The place where those who entered the doors grew by leaps and bounds, then exited so much better for it. I called it White-Hood's grow-and-go formula. What made this formula different, tons and tons of *care*!

What Does *Care* Look Like?

✓ active and respectful listening
✓ keeping promises
✓ never closing the door
✓ unafraid of bigness
✓ loving and nurturing the students
✓ understanding that we can mentor parents
✓ programming for the whole child (interests, hobbies, strengths, weaknesses, topical issues, mindfulness, growth)
✓ patience, love, tolerance, and prayer

I thought, *It's amazing to be on this journey.* I could have been apologetic and contrite. But I have to admit it—I was proud and honored to be on a journey that would lead me to a new school of my making. I turned to God's promises in Genesis 12:1–3, "I will bless those who bless you," and Philippians 4:19, "And my God will supply all my needs according to his riches in glory by Christ Jesus." There was no doubt about it. *God is* powerful, compassionate, wise, faithful, and loving.

Wearing God's armor, I chose to be resolute, a change agent—a researcher and an inventor of ways of doing things! In this new role, I wore business suits every day and heels. But I kept three pair of tennis shoes in my closet at school.

The new school was a visually stunning facility! I had a large office—a beautiful space to work—conference room, testing office, and a health room that we renamed after a famous African American doctor. The classrooms were efficient, well-designed, and student-friendly. The work stations resembled laboratories. The library was resource-rich! We had computers in every classroom and a technology café. All classrooms were equipped with smart boards and televisions, sound equipment, etc.

In addition, I was fortunate enough to recruit, interview, and on-board some of the best teachers in the state. In fact, we had a diverse workforce that led us to more ideas and innovation, which benefits students. Staff, parents, and students helped write the school's core values. We were forced to be intentional about everything we did as a team. I told the team that "eyes were upon us." I thrived and cried with joy and thankfulness. My journey through the process of opening the school was based on some extremely important scriptures.

White-Hood's Guiding Scriptures

- Wisdom (James 1:5)
- Hope (1 Thessalonians 1:3)
- Hebrews 4:16
- Romans 3:23
- Philemon 1:4
- Proverbs 1:5
- Psalm 73:24
- Proverbs 3:6
- Psalm 119:105
- Matthew 5:18
- Ephesians 6:1–3
- 2 Timothy 1:7
- Isaiah 41:10

Sometimes I floundered, but God was the answer. He supported me as I became aware of myself (decision process, gracefulness, ability to manage my emotions, empathy, referring to the Word). When I did not know what or how to pray, I found the answer in my Bible.

Another story. Once I was trying to be cute and wore sandals during a building tour and accidently step on a piece of medal, I thought I would lose my toe but didn't. God was the answer. When I slipped in my new office and dislocated my shoulder, God was the answer. He was trying to tell me something—"Be careful, follow the rules. They were not made to be broken. They were made to protect." I savored God's love, care, and protection.

Building a Team to Open the New Middle School

One staff member commented, "Every time I turn around, you have a new idea, Dr. White-Hood."

We chuckled. I knew that I needed to *slow my roll*. My devotion, energy, and excitement literarily knocked me out of my chair.

I really didn't want a team that would rubber-stamp my ideas. I did not want my team to be silly-putty in my hands. I needed to rely on diversity that provided a greater range of talent. If we were to be a team, a family, and a group of collaborators, some of our processes would expose some ugly truths about all of us. For instance, I would need the courage to be unpopular and say what I needed to say sometimes. This was my truth, my reality.

Nevertheless, I wanted our leadership team to be "our school in miniature." The team would reflect the culture of the school—a culture of belonging. Our team would model certain characteristics—be socially responsive, trustworthy, well-respected, humanistic, yet evidence-driven, and accountable. We also knew that drawing students from diverse communities would help us use different lens to solve challenges, operate our school, and make it strong. This would be a value add.

Our school would celebrate differences, include of all teachers, parents, and students from underrepresented groups (our non-contiguous communities). We would need to craft affirmations and micro-affirmations, provide continuous professional development to help everyone grow and learn more, galvanize and engage parents from all communities, provide students with the resources they need to be successful, give students and parents choices and a voice.

I returned to my dream of a beautifully diverse school—teachers, students, and parents creating a mosaic of understanding, peace, learning, and growth. I asked a few teachers to help me by visiting feeder schools to meet with parents. I wanted them to know, see, feel the vision of diversity, the power of working together, the richness of our new school.

I asked the art and technology teacher to design flyers, banners, and brochures to recruit new teachers. We visited the University of Maryland, University of the District of Columbia, Bowie State University, and others. Our goal was to meet with graduating seniors who wanted to be teachers. I reached out to national associations to recruit potential teachers.

I incorporated a diverse interview panel to ensure that candidates chosen solely based on suitability for the position: credentials, skills and knowledge of content, enthusiasm for teaching diverse and sometime under-resourced students. I wanted to provide sensitivity training to adjust perspectives and coaching or mentoring training to sure up hard and soft skills. We needed to be creative when recruiting staff. Ideas and strategies flowed like water! Out-of-the-box thinking was plentiful! I dotted all i's and crossed all t's by seeking approval from my superiors.

Our leadership team would be civically engaged in the school district's efforts. So as a new school, we had a lot to figure out. Just how would we balance the multiple narratives? How would we anticipate what was to come? How would we borrow some of the best ideas from local school districts experiencing success? What external forces will affect the new school? Do we want to serve or expect to be served?

This work was a calling! I wanted to see our school in the MSDE story of excellent schools. How would we obtain that kind of excellence? As the founding principal, I knew that I would have to seek mentoring moments from several outstanding leaders like the mathematics supervisor, magnet office supervisor, and my doctoral adviser. I wanted to be professional, credible, thoughtful, and forthright as a founding principal, asking deep, penetrating, and compelling questions, while growing in the process. I remembered what a mentor said, "The most dangerous part of a job is when its half done. People tend to give up from exhaustion." I leaned into God's love!

I depended upon my first assistant principal—the one who followed me from my first school. I never gave up on her, and she never gave up on me. I used my grandmother's mantra: "A new broom sweeps clean, but an old one knows the corners," and my assistant principal knew the corners, the walls, the halls, and the steps of my thinking. Of this work, we termed "creating a legendary school."

The Biggest Challenge—School Shootings!

There were stories and accounts on every news channel and in every newspaper. These were volatile and fear-filled times. We began having crisis drills and emergency drills and shelter-in-place practices. Since our building had walls of glass as part of its design, the students expressed their fears daily. I was afraid but refused to show it. I turned to the *Word*; move from *fear* to *fear not*. That helped me guide our school through to the other side.

Commentary

CHAPTER 3

**Dreams Do Come True: Opening
a New Middle School**

First day

The curtain was up, and the spotlight was on *me!*

Do I want to be a boss or a leader? I wanted to be a leader. I wanted to build something special, not complicated but meaningful and full of hope.

My past was transformative; my relationships with teachers, students, and parents shaped me, and yet, I, Marian White-Hood, was still evolving, accelerating, and now glistening.

There is a lot to unpack in this chapter.

I began with a *middle school dedication*. The team planned the event, and I handled my mom. I shopped for the perfect dress, shoes that she could walk in, and a summary of all that I had experienced (just in case she wanted to brag). The entire dedication was a different experience. It was evidence of what collaboration, respect, and dedication can do.

We invited parents, community members, legislators, and members of the superintendent's staff. The children wore their school uniforms, and the student government members served as tour guides.

Countdown to Opening Day

communications—newsletters, flyers, brochures
internal design—showcased giant mural of Dr. EE Just
library designs—stained-glass doors
research
teacher profiles—prepared by teachers, edited and posted
creative scheduling
directory
monthly staff-meeting calendar
bus duty
teacher handbook
student handbook
signage

The morning before school opened, we met at 5:00 a.m.! With holy water in hand, several leadership team members marched through the school sprinkling drops of water at every door; reading scripture; and praying for peace, love, and learning.

Numerous activities were planned. There were three open houses each year, student orientation, on-boarding staff, sign-ups for clubs, second-cup-of-coffee morning meetings with parents, school-improvement team meetings, etc. Several students requested an after-school prayer club.

I received calls and inquiries from principals and administrators from other districts. The questions facing me were immense. It's important to note that I felt as though I was still in the learner's seat. I was still curious…curious about the technology, student body, my new teachers, parents, and community members. In addition, I met with parents and responded to phone calls and emails *75 percent* of the day. My goal was to be the best version of myself for all stakeholders. And I could not have achieved that goal by myself.

Our two assistant principals were phenomenal women! They had duties yet were eager to do more. They were extremely competent, supported each other, and held my hand through the ups and downs. (Side bar: two of the assistant principals are now award-winning principals in other New York and Columbia, Maryland, districts.)

The leadership team was committed to opening the school in a safe and academically strong way. My dynamic team understood my passion and vision for the school. They did not disappoint! The team consisted of the following:

> 2 assistant principals (seventh and eighth grade)
> 2 counselors (seventh and eighth grade)
> 6 department chairs (mathematics, English, social studies, science, physical education, creative arts, technology)
> 4 parents
> 4 students
> ----------------
> 18 total

Growing the Leadership Team

For the most part, the team members complemented one another and represented a beautiful mosaic, rich in knowledge, skills, determination, and character. I remember one team member who frequently reminded us that it's easy to sign up to join a team but not easy to stay with it. He would speak up at meetings, saying: "Don't be discouraged!" Three words that we used throughout the years. His thinking and inspirational messages resonate with me even today.

There were numerous lessons to be learned about growing a leadership team. Many times the team is misunderstood, and members feel unappreciated. A few staff members—I call the *negatives*—will try to impugn the reputation of the team. As enemies of the process, they may look for things to trip members up. As the principal, I take my eyes off my own feelings (myself) and put them on the Lord, who knows me best

First-Four Years' Activities

- Saturday school
- winter-break school
- summer camp
- summer bridge for incoming seventh graders
- Rose Court
- gentlemen's association
- tech café
- teacher articulation
- feeder and middle school conferences
- academic banquets
- quarterly honor roll
- 4.0 club or 3.0 club
- testing and assessment and celebrations
- ten-point program

My four years at the school were amazing! I met many people and learned many things. I'm reminded of this text:

People Come into Your Life for a Reason, a Season, or a Lifetime

"People come into your life for a reason, a season, or a lifetime." When you figure out which one it is, you will know what to do for each person. When someone is in your life for a REASON…it is usually to meet a need you have expressed. They have come to assist you through a difficulty, to provide you with guidance and support, to aid you physically, emotionally, or spiritually. They may seem like a godsend, and they are! They are there for the reason you need them to be. Then, without any wrongdoing on your part or at an inconvenient time, this person will say or do something to bring the relationship to an end. Sometimes they die. Sometimes they walk away. Sometimes they act up and force you to take a stand. What we must realize is that our need has been met; our desire fulfilled; their work is done. The prayer you sent up has been answered. And now it is time to move on.

When people come into your life for a SEASON...

Because your turn has come to share, grow, or learn. They bring you an experience of peace or make you laugh. They may teach you something you have never done. They usually give you an unbelievable amount of joy. Believe it! It is real! But only for a season.

LIFETIME relationships teach you lifetime lessons, things you must build upon in order to have a solid emotional foundation. Your job is to accept the lesson, love the person, and put what you have learned to use in all other relationships and areas of your life.

—Author Unknown

I was guided by the "North Star:"

school district's mission – my vision as principal + students' and stakeholders' values = my North Star

By the end of my fourth year, I felt a sense of peace. Toward the end of my third year at the school, I knew that I needed a mental tune-up; we all did. I needed to refresh my thoughts because it's easy to get fatigued in education. So, I took some spiritual walks, which helped me stay excited about leading. I spent the summer building a leadership library full of spiritual materials, inspiring texts, self-care books and tapes.

Commentary

CHAPTER 4

Leadership, Not My Way!

The superintendent heard about my Saturday school program—a program that was not funded. Teachers volunteered to tutor children on Saturday mornings, and I used school-improvement funds to pay for the transportation for children.

I received a call notifying me that I was being promoted. Where would I go from here? I would be based at the Board of Education's Magnet Office (renamed FOCUS Office), to plan and implement supplemental-education programs in middle schools around the school district. These programs were available on Saturday mornings, and certified teachers were hired to serve as site directors and teachers.

Although I learned a lot, the drive to the office was a cold one. My new supervisor was tough to work for and work with. I felt constrained, conflicted, disrespected, fearful, and sometimes dehumanized. I felt as though I was the peon surrounded by negativity. Meetings were toxic. Many days, I cried on the way home. Was God trying to tell me something?

In addition, I missed the pitter-patter of students' feet, visiting physical education class, observing teachers, meeting with parents, and the whole "principal thing."

Moreover, the new position was changing my posture. I felt like I lost my edge…was less confident and troubled. From where I sat, everything deteriorated. This was a different reality! Can you love a school district and critique it honestly? Things felt dark, too dark.

When I learned that the principal of my old middle school was leaving at the end of the year, I requested a transfer back to the school. I was a fighter, but I had no strength or desire to stay there. If there was ever a time to make a change, this was it! I remembered the famous words: "The principalship is the best job in education!" God gave me an assignment and helped me get back on the road to reach my destination.

What helped me make the transition: *forgiveness* (Ephesians 1:7) and *victory* (2 Corinthians 2:14).

Commentary

CHAPTER 5

The Worse Time: Retirement

I returned to the middle school that I founded. It was my place—a place I called *school.*

My love for the school and the principalship was unwavering. God helped me realize that I truly am who I say I am; I'll do what I say I will do. I will never deny *him.*

I was proud and privileged to take on the responsibilities of the principalship. Over the next two years, I upgraded the processes and procedures that were needed to move the school forward. I addressed state and local testing requirements, parent engagement, school climate, and the unique needs and interests on pre- and early adolescents.

In 2007, my mother became ill. I tried to balance my professional school life with my personal and family life. There were times when I fell to my knees, praying for guidance and direction. These scriptures helped:

> But if any of you lacks wisdom, let him ask
> of God, who gives to all generously and without
> reproach, and it will be given to him. (James 1:5)

> For You are my rock and my fortress; For
> Your name's sake, You will lead me and guide me.
> (Psalm 31:3)

> Trust in the Lord with all your heart and do
> not lean on your own understanding. In all your
> ways acknowledge Him, and He will make your
> paths straight. (Proverbs 3:5–6)

I'm reminded of a song. Not sure of the title but it goes like this: "After you have done all you can /you just stand. God has a purpose/ Stand/Stand/Pray."

That summer, I knew that I needed to retire when I attended a principals' retreat and found that eighteen of my former teachers were now principals or administrators. They were young, smart, innovative, competent, and highly skilled.

I retired to take care of my mom, but she passed on to glorious heaven in January 2008.

Mama died; I was overwhelmed with grief. She put her trust in Christ. Her last words: "I may not make it, but I want to let the doctors help others through me." It was her unselfish love of others; she signed the consent for surgery but did not make it through. I was devastated.

My PTA president helped plan her funeral. Once again, I found myself bedridden in a fetal position for weeks. Shortly after, I had a horrible colon accident! Colonoscopy gone wrong! God knows how to get your attention!

I lived with my twin brother for six months, had four surgeries, and had a pity party of one until my brother ordered me to "get on your knees and pray that God has use for you, here." So that's exactly what I did. I struggled, crawled out of the bed, got on my knees, and prayed.

From my daily reading of the Word, I began to see a new reality. I begin looking for another job, partnering with God. Confident and with a bold posture, I went to an interview and landed a position in a charter school. I would be the director of academics in an alternative charter school. But what if? Rooted in a deep revelation of who God said I was, I accepted the new assignment. Hebrews 10:19–22.

I planned to stay in the position for a year. But some words resonated with me: "I know what you have need of." They were words to meditate on. I remembered what Pastor Joel Olsten says, "Rule your day!" This assignment came from God, and I was more blessed in the second part of life. The school needed me, and I need it.

Commentary

CHAPTER 6

A New Journey: Charter School

An Alternative

I heard a song by Reba McEntire "Somehow You Do" (2021). The words were "When you think it's the end of the road, it's because you don't know where the road is leading to." Thank you, Father...for blessing me with that song."

As director of academics of five campuses, I did not like driving across the city—parking tickets, speeding tickets, and meter maids, oh no!

The Charter School Experience

The high school charter was no picnic! I found myself calling out, "Jesus, please take the wheel!" I knew that there might be some thunderstorms, but I had my poncho on; my umbrella up. Things that I learned in the school district served me well. In fact, I could not have made it in the charter world if it had not been for my *formal training and experiences* in the public-school system. The one could not have happened without the other. Becoming a charter school leader was, in fact, my greatest turning point!

After the first month, I knew that leadership will shine when you are where you belong.

Welcome to the Charter World, Oh My!

First things first. I didn't know what I did not know. It's time to stretch and grow!

But I almost needed another "head to take in all the new things" I learned about charter schools in general and an alternative school, specifically. For instance, I remember greeting the students at the door, walking down the hallway. I saw a female and greeted her with two words *good morning*. The girl "rolled her eyes" and made a profane comment. I followed her down the hall and asked her to stop. I wanted to talk with her. Enter Dr. Kamal, who quickly motioned me to talk with him. "Dr. White-Hood, the girl did not have a good morning. She is homeless and probably slept on the streets of DC," explained Dr. Kamal. I will never forget his entrance into my life. As a leader and highly respected director, Dr. Kamal Wright Cunningham taught me many lessons about the world of alternative education. After several weeks, I was able to build a strong relationship with the girl who graduated after several years.

Lesson learned: the leader needs to know about the behaviors of the students he or she is responsible for—positive and negative. Just as I learned the names of all the students in my earlier schools, I needed to know all about the students in the alternative school including challenges, growth areas, talents, and interests. I need to know about their struggles, backgrounds, and home lives.

The students were quite remarkable, different from students I worked with. They were streetwise, strong, and resilient. They loved, respected, and appreciated the counselors. There seemed to be a shared understanding that was uniquely different from public schools—the role of the counselor and the role of the student.

The five campuses were in Ward 7/8. The students suffered from widespread poverty when there seemed to be economic prosperity in DC. The fact that the students came to school in rain, snow, blizzard weather was emancipatory. I had never been in a school like this one, never worked with students like these, and with issues like large student population, court involvement, teen parents, unemployment, poverty, hunger. Many of the students were in the special education program and had IEPs that were not being implemented. The ninth-grade population was extremely large—students were retained for three to four years in ninth grade.

The counselors and teachers focused on a social justice theme and designed programs like college prep and group. I could see the goodness of God in ways I had never seen before.

I always thought that charter schools were not important; they robbed public education of funds that they needed. After visiting classrooms, talking to teachers and students, I was surely immune to apathy and was unafraid. Just how does change happens? I was excited to dig into it!

Back in the Saddle

What would be my process?

This was a failing school…an alternative school. How would I shift the paradigm?

How would I show the staff who I was…what I was about?

How would I inspire and identify leadership team members to keep working hard? Focus on team dynamics?

How would I leverage myself to help the teachers and staff?

What would my leadership style look like?

What professional knowledge would I build upon?

What about data? What points would I need? When? How? What would be the system for managing data? Utilizing data?

What evidence would we need?

How would I evaluate the process?

The leader in White-Hood was back! I *listened*…I got to know what people needed and wanted and that included the community, parents, students, and teachers. I began pulling together a leadership team, sharing ideas, and focusing on *growing the staff*. I realized that the school was resourceless, so I began to network, arranging local and state visitation.

What I was suggesting was extraordinary for an alternative education. I chose a slogan for administrators from the movie *Drumline*—"One band…one sound!" I worked with the executive director and her staff to write grants that would support professional growth and expand the leadership team to include a mathematics coach, English coach, college-going and career director, etc. The team worked with teachers to develop classroom commitments and promises, small rewards and reinforcement and opportunities to *brag* on the students.

I knew that I had some growing to do in the area of alternative education. I was thirsty for books, conferences, videotapes, anything that would shed light on the topic. For instance, once I heard Sheryl J. Denbo say, "There are several complex and varied reasons African American students underachieve." The words resonated with me over and over. I was *obsessed*!

I wanted the MAPCS to become a community of *hope*…a family that was value-driven. Two campuses were located in a dangerous section of DC. In fact, there were at least three cars broken in to each week. So I worked with the leadership team to ramp up safety; build relationships; introduce holistic, therapeutic mental-health strategies. We wanted to have an impact on the students by teaching social skills, empathy, and respect.

We were awarded grants, and we were able to plan school-based professional development conferences for all campuses.

- the whole child
- evidence-based practices
- family engagement
- teacher mentors
- trauma-informed practices
- social and emotional learning
- blended learning
- special education

- *grit*
- twenty-first-century skills
- CTE

Professional development was meticulously documented. What we offered the teachers and staff would ultimately have a broad-based impact on the students. Encouraging souls daily became a lifestyle.

Leadership Roles Emerged

Instead of suspending and expelling students every day, I create a position that I called hearing officer, which I personally held without pay. We wanted to put in the hands of all learners the skills, knowledge, and resources needed to be successful. To do this, we needed to increase attendance and punctuality. My goal was to keep students in school by rewriting the code of conduct using restorative-justice strategies, in-school suspension, and corrective feedback, and ramp up the special education department, ensuring that IEPs were compliant.

One day, I received a visit from the chairman of the MAPCS Board. He was concerned about enrollment and the possibility of not meeting the DCPCSB requirements and mandates. He stated firmly, "You don't want to have to tell a hundred people that they do not have a job anymore because the campuses closed."

This let me know that my position was more than that of academic director. I was the "leader in charge of everything" and reporting to the MAPCS Board and executive director. So my next step was to observe, attend charter meetings to understand the *agency* (charter world).

Next Steps

- Have morning meetings
- Infuse soft skills (expressive skills) into the curriculum
- Create a ten-point plan that included attendance and punctuality checks, involvement in activities
- Identify ways to support content knowledge
- Ensure the engagement of hard histories and difficult conversations
- Promote the MAPCS mission and social justice themes

Another Leadership Role

An assistant principal of one of the campuses was appointed to a principal position. After five months, she was terminated because she was not able to meet her enrollment target. (Note: charter schools run on enrollment dollars.)

I found myself assuming the position of acting principal for six months. I had only been at the school for approximately five months. So I brainstormed all the duties of a principal, reviewed personnel records, and engaged several school leaders in dialogue, asking questions about philosophy. I had my eye on the mathematics department chair. But she was not interested in the assistant principal position. She was committed to improving mathematics outcomes, especially in calculus and geometry.

I trusted the feelings that God put in my mind and on my heart. God never fails me. My evidence: the sixty-six books in the Bible. After much convincing, the head of the mathematics department became my assistant principal.

What happened to the assistant principal? Later, the new assistant principal became principal of a successful charter school in the city. After a few years, she was selected to be a principal of a charter school located on a college campus. Within five years, she was selected as the NASSP Principal of the Year for city.

Aspiring Principal

- spiritual
- servant leader
- energetic
- wise and keen thinker
- student-focused
- knowledge of content
- high visibility and exposure
- data-driven
- with leadership qualities
- course requirement

The what ifs were running through my mind. By the end of the day, I knew that I was highly blessed, and God had the steering wheel. I thanked God for this math teacher turned administrator. I continue to pray, "Father, how grateful I am. I know that the only way to live is through you. I love you, in Jesus's name. Amen."

Leadership Roles Emerged

- chief academic officer
- acting high school principal
- hearing officer
- interim recruiter (HR)
- curriculum specialist
- grant writer
- director of academics

When I was able to recruit and hire someone from the charter board to become the principal of one of our campuses, I was ecstatic!

I was able to put more time and energy into the director-of-academics role.

One story that I want to share deals with the new principal who had an excellent rapport with students (court-involved, teen parents, with special needs, etc.)

One Monday morning, the principal learned that one of his male students—a boy he mentored—was shot execution-style. The principal screamed and wept in the hall. Within days, he visited the family, planned grief-counseling sessions, offered funds, and planned for staff and students to attend the funeral services.

Another significant story: there was a basketball game with another high school. Parents and players began fighting in the street after the game. The principal was disappointed.

These stories and many more haunted me. I recall crying at the altar during our church service, then giving a testimony. Hurting hurts!

For seven long years, I dedicated myself to the five campuses because students, staff, and parents needed nourishment. There was sorrow upon sorrow, prolonged emotional sorrow. The MAPCS family experienced traumatic events two to three times a week. I played Kirk Franklin's tapes over and over and prayed to take the *shackles off* so that the school could impact the students and their families in positive ways.

When planning with the team, I made certain to solicit different points of view. I had "think partners" and did not have much pushback.

But I stayed there…I stayed at the table, loving the staff and students, understanding that the greater the risk, the greater the reward. I learned what was possible for me.

First things first: since I loved to be close to the students and teachers, I collaborated with the assistant principal to create a tiered observation schedule that included learning circles, walk-throughs, informal preobservation conferences, informal observations and post-observation conferences, collegial partnerships, and coaching. This plan would ensure that I was near to each student's heart and those who supported him or her.

The highways and byways of my journey increased my perceptions, perspectives, and practices. I was on the road to success. It was an *exhilarating ride*!

White-Hood Serves as Acting Principal of a Ward 7/8 Charter School

Description of the Role

- Implements the school's charter in collaboration with the school's board of directors and the authorizing institution;
- Provides instructional leadership for the alignment of curriculum, instruction, and assessment through the purposeful observation and evaluation of teachers;
- Establishes and communicates standards for students including their academic performance;
- Assesses school's practices and procedures continuously and adjusts them to support the diverse learning needs of students;
- Assumes responsibility for the health, safety, and welfare of the students, staff, and visitors;
- Infuses the school culture with the school's mission;
- Models positive character virtues and habits and assists students in developing positive moral and performance character attributes;
- Oversees the financial management of the school, including development of the annual budget; oversees the management of accounts payable and accounts receivable; approves payroll; makes provisions of required financial reports to the board, district, and state; and ensures the annual financial audit is completed in a timely manner;
- Collaborates and clearly communicates with parents and guardians, all members of the school community and other educators;

- Develops, articulates, and implements a vision of learning that is shared and supported by the school community;
- Builds professional learning communities to nurture and sustain a school culture and instructional program conducive to accelerated student achievement;
- Acts ethically and according to professional norms to promote each student's academic success and well-being;
- Seeks and engages in professional activities that foster leadership development; building the capacity of the assistant principal and other aspiring leaders;
- Demonstrates integrity, fairness, mutual respect, and high ethical standards; works cooperatively and interacts positively with students, staff, and community exercising courtesy and discretion; serves as a role model for staff and students;
- Complies with all board policies and operating procedures; and
- Performs other duties as assigned.

I drew strength from the scriptures and songs by Yolanda Adams, Steve Crown's "You Are Great" (2015), and Jennifer Hudson's "Fix Me Jesus" (2014). I felt *his* presence within me and was inspired and challenged. I prayed daily, "God please help your children."

When I left the school, one of my principals whispered to me, "Wisdom! It felt good knowing that you were always here to guide us." And God was there to *guide me*.

Lessons Learned

I learned that you cannot underestimate the breath and the depth of what God can do for you. I eventually became the chief academic officer, and I stayed at the school for almost eight years.

Commentary

54

CHAPTER 7

Turning Around Lives Through Organizational Change
Potomac Preparatory Public Charter School

The executive director hosted a farewell dinner for me in a downtown restaurant. At first, I did not want to attend, but God sent me on my way. I enjoyed the food, friends, and frivolity. As I walked to the parking lot, something began to change.

I felt a shadow slowly masking me. It was due to unresolved pain of the past, unresolved hurt caused by what-if questions. *What would be my next step? What road would I take?*

The next day, I was on the road when I received a phone call from a representative of another charter school. I was offered an interview! The school was on the charter school docket to close; it needed a principal, a leader. After learning as much as I could about the school from the trustees, I realized that I would need a leadership team. I would also need to review the data, qualitative and quantitative; achievement benchmarks; the school's improvement plan; articles about the school's charter—*how it began*; and meet with parents, students, and teachers.

What I Knew Moving Forward

- high teacher turnover
- lower teacher expectations

- disproportionate expulsion and suspension policy
- contradictions
  1. close relationships
  2. disrespectful climate
  3. intervention plan

I reviewed the files of every staff member. But there were challenges. As I reviewed files, teachers were quitting left and right. As I met with administrators, I found that several had no real experience or credentials for the position.

I retitled administrative positions and created job descriptions. Once administrators were recruited, we began to meet. My goal: *relationship building.* I wanted to know the strengths, talents, experiences, and growth points of each administrator. I made it clear that I did not want dishonesty or rubber-stamping! We created a slogan, "Ignite the passion!"

Then I began to galvanize parents, who, for the most part, were committed to the school. They would be a strong part of the fabric that I was weaving. So they met with me in focus groups.

I knew that I would have to be keener than I had been in the past. I didn't want anything to erode the relationship I had with the Lord. He would fill my spine with steel and give me unshakable hope and strength. I had to *hold my head high and walk through fire that was burning.* The charter-board climate was very unnerving. There were meetings, phone calls, emails, and a barrage of questions about the school—a school that I was rebranding, recreating, and reforming. There was a lack of empathy on the city charter board's part. I felt as though our charter was being "gunned." Were we entrapped?

Every decision that I made as principal had to be *made based on spiritual reality.* My mind was in overdrive. "The choice you make, makes you…the choice you make, makes you…the choice you make, makes you."

My survival would depend on my leadership skills. I depended upon (1) my *beliefs* or what was in my head and (2) my *convictions* or what was in my heart. I dived deep into the data to uncover the following:

- The school needed *top-notch*, high-quality teachers who were highly versed in the curriculum.
- Teachers needed more support so that they could successfully deliver instruction.
- We needed to do these:
  o Identify types of parent involvement and train parents
  o Create an academic ambience
  o Develop discipline alternatives
  o Attendance
  o Tutorials
  o Homework help
  o Interventions
- We needed to improve special-education services
- We need to create a professional development plan that included triaging and tiering teachers.
- We needed to design an acceleration plan!

Deep in my heart, I knew that I would have to dive into every child's story. I needed to be brave! Would I be able to meet their needs? How would I ensure that teachers would identify each students' greatest needs and match them with the best practices? This required teachers to identify a rich repertoire of teaching approaches. It meant that teachers would have to support social and emotional learning, encourage collaboration and teamwork, build and sustain positive relationships with students, parents, and colleagues. This would not be easy. *But God…*

There were some mistakes I made along the way, so I was always asking Jesus to forgive me of my sins.

And forgive us our trespasses, as we forgive those who trespass against us, and lead us not into temptation, but deliver us from evil.

—The Lord's Prayer

I went into seclusion and designed an incentive plan for teachers, one for parents, and one for students. During the month of May, before I actually stepped in as principal, I conducted a study of the school.

Presentation to the District Charter Board
Qualitative Study and Entry Plan—Potomac PCS
Marian White-Hood, Principal
June 2014

As part of my entry plan, I collected data from various sources. Methods of investigation used included but were not limited to

- parent focus-group session,
- parent meet and greet,
- teacher interviews,
- staff meet and greet,
- leadership team member interviews,
- comparison to national benchmarks and best practices,
- collection and analysis of relevant data,
- review of multiple documents,
- collection and review of numerous related research articles,
- online research,
- pre-K interviews, and
- grade 6 focus group.

Initial Findings

The improvement of academic performance is recognized by Potomac PSC board members and some staff members as an urgent and critical issue for the school to address. On behalf of the board, this reviewer uncovered many root causes for poor academic performance. For example, there are challenges for the both students and faculty, including high levels of teacher turnover, students busing over several miles each day, and a weak operational structure.

On the other hand, there are some positive findings in the area of instruction and particularly in the high level of care that teachers show toward students each day. There are pockets of good instructional practice, but this is inconsistent across the school. The preschool team, for instance, models high standards, collaboration, and parent involvement. In addition, the special-education department is functioning well, and compliance issues are minor. However, there have been several substitute teachers for grade 3, and classroom-climate issues are numerous.

While there may be effective management and operational systems used at Lighthouse, these are not apparent at the Potomac site. It is apparent that the following areas require immediate attention:

1. Processes and protocols to create efficiency
2. New organizational and management efficiency structures that can provide improved support to the school
3. Improved communication tools and processes so that the system is transparent to its stakeholders, and all staff members remain informed and able to collaborate with one another.

In addition, instructional leadership is *not* rigorous enough in pursuit of high-quality teaching. Therefore, students' varied academic needs are not fully met in every classroom. It is also apparent that parents are positive about the school but are not involved in decision-making processes.

Findings from In-Depth Study

Based on the deep-dive protocol including a review of documents, parent-focus-group data, and teacher-interview data, the following areas were found to be problematic:

1. Strategic Planning and Implementation
   A *strategic plan* to support the urgent and sustainable change does not exist. This type of plan would capture

the energy and passion of stakeholders as they commit to do their best for *the* students they serve. This plan can be aligned to school, charter, or district needs. It can be realistic about the issues the school may face when bringing about accelerated improvement. It can be a living document, vividly influencing the daily work of those who will implement it.

Similarly, the plan must include the use of data and clearly define key issues. The plan must include ongoing evaluation of each strategy's impact and provide a framework for deciding what needs to be done next.

The Potomac plan must be easily understood by all stakeholders and facilitated by individuals who are entirely committed to its success—parents, teachers, leaders, and board members. These individuals must collaborate with one another regularly and display a willingness to challenge and be challenged while focusing on learner outcomes. Moreover, the plan must be a relevant and useful tool that can be monitored and implemented with fidelity.

2. Teaching and Learning

From the PCSB Qualitative Site Review and classroom observations, it is apparent that the following areas must be addressed:

- Targeted supports that are aligned to well-articulated priorities to meet the needs of the learners;
- Curriculum, instruction, and assessments that are aligned to the common core standards, implemented in ways that engage and challenge all students to think critically, communicate, and demonstrate their learning in various ways;
- Professional development that is tiered and delivered, monitored, and evaluated in ways that ensure teacher quality so that all students can learn and apply key concept; and

- Access to programs, services, and opportunities that prepare students for the next level, which will ultimately ensure college and career readiness.

3. Communications and Community Engagement

A clear mission and vision need to be outlined and supported through strong leadership and strategic focus. In addition, issues around staffing and organization need to be addressed to improve productivity and efficiency and to foster a more positive work environment. Similarly, a clearly articulated set of processes and protocols will guide the work of the school. All these are important to stakeholders but must be broadly communicated. Thus, a communications plan that includes key strategies that are aligned to the school goals is needed. This plan will improve the image of the school through a concerted rebranding effort.

4. Operations

While there has been some change, upheaval, and instability in the area of operations, there has been a commitment among some nonteaching personnel to continuous improvement, and despite numerous challenges, the school continues to run at a normal pace. By focusing on school operations, Potomac will be armed to ensure student safety, decrease teacher turnover, promote parent involvement, focus on whole-child tenets, and improve achievement for every student.

5. Organizational Efficiency and Effectiveness

A review of student achievement and performance data suggests a need to closely evaluate the organizational structures and efficiency of the school, given the continued stagnant performance of both the elementary and middle school on state assessment. The current system has created poor communication among grade levels, divisiveness among staff members, and can also be attributed to teacher turnover. It is apparent that the heavy lifting and work is not being done efficiently. The aforementioned areas must be functioning well in order for the school to operate at peak performance.

Summary

Three (3) overarching themes for improvement emerged across reports:

1. Strategic focus and leadership—the school needs to engage in intensive organizational development that includes emphasis on
   - clarity of roles and responsibilities;
   - development of a strong mission and vision, goals, and values; and
   - changing the culture to one that is focused on supporting the school and on impacting student achievement, which means creating a strong academic ambience.
2. Organization and staffing—an analysis of work functions and roles must be conducted. The staffing needs of all grades must be examined closely for increases or reductions. New protocols for organizational efficiency can provide more clarity and consistent communication about the responsibilities of various departments, including teaching and learning.
3. Processes and protocols—because of the challenges around school effectiveness, the school will benefit from adopting an internal performance excellence management system (PEMS). Parent, teacher, and student representatives can join administrators each month as they audit processes and protocols for effectiveness. The PEMS reports will drive improvements.

Team members will work together to solve problems, improve processes, and search for the best way to ensure quality. That means that activities must be aligned to the mission and goals of the school;

cooperation and collaboration are standard operating procedure; standards are high but are simplified by processes and procedures; staff are supported in their work by tool kits; human-capital programs must be instituted that develop staff members and foster a disciplined professional culture; and the school must operate using turnaround practices.

Next Steps

It is recommended that all the stakeholders *target* eight (8) goals for 2014–2015:

- Goal 1—Ensure *teaching and learning* produces students ready to advance to the next level with the ultimate goal of reaching college or landing a career.
- Goal 2—Transform community trust through transparent *communications*. Create opportunities to listen broadly and deeply to a diverse group of stakeholders in an effort to transform community trust and build relationships.
- Goal 3—Create an *organizational structure* staffed with a skilled leadership team centered on enhancing teaching and learning.
- Goal 4—*Align resources* to school priorities and goals.
- Goal 5—Establish a *leadership team* of educational administrators, practitioners, and stakeholders to help determine the next steps as it relates to key area of school operations.
- Goal 6—Conduct *regular audits and reviews* of all aspects of the school—i.e., operations, teaching, parent engagement.
- Goal 7—Seek *support from the board* to maximize efforts through trust, accountability, and high professional standards.
- Goal 8—Work with the board to *determine mission and charter goals*; communicate with students, staff, and parents.

Assurances

I. The new principal will…

- Schedule strategic-planning sessions
- Identify and develop key priorities in the plan, which will lead to transformational change
- Define the strategies and actions to be undertaken to meet those priorities
- Identify the resources required to enable efficient and effective implementation
- Develop and implement effective processes to ensure the outputs of the plan are accurate, high-quality, and delivered on time
- Define and establish systems for monitoring, evaluating, reviewing, and revising the plan on a monthly basis to ensure that the strategies and actions are having the desired impact
- Establish effective communication and engagement structures for all key stakeholders associated with the plan
- Monitor time and scope of the plan to ensure progress is occurring at the appropriate pace
- Ensure ongoing professional development

Impact on Teachers and Staff

1. Improved teacher quality
2. Teacher sustainability
3. Teacher productivity and performance
4. Teacher professionalism and accountability
5. Improved professional culture and staff cohesiveness

Expected Outcomes for Potomac Public Charter School

- Create conditions in the school to accelerate student learning
- Focus the work of teacher teams on the instructional core
- Train the leadership team on planning of school improvement
- Identify and support initiatives that are working while moving off programs that do not produce results
- Students will achieve.

II. The new principal will…

- Establish an effective classroom observation process and cycle
- Create an effective leadership observation process and cycle
- Improve leadership and observation capacity within the school
- Provide leaders with the confidence and skills to observe lessons, analyze student work, and make sound judgments about teaching and learning
- Develop lesson observation and feedback skills that will contribute to the consistent teaching and learning standards across the schools
- Use data to personalize the teaching and learning process while ensuring productive student engagement

Impact on Teachers and Staff

1. Learn how data are collected and recorded to make judgments
2. Become more confident in making those judgments
3. Provide productive and developmental feedback to teachers
4. Better evaluate student learning through examining student work and performance data

5. Collect a strong evidence-based data to support the teacher-evaluation system
6. Students will achieve.

Expected Outcomes for Potomac Public Charter School
Use the wealth of available data more effectively at the classroom level to ensure lessons are closely aligned to the full range of students' learning needs and enable rapid and targeted responses to changes in their needs. Students will achieve.

III. The new principal will…

- Improve the assessment-for-learning process
- Ensure effective feedback to students and parents
- Promote active involvement of students in their own learning
- Recognize the profound influence that assessment has on self-esteem and motivation
- Help others be able to assess themselves and understand how to improve
- Promote inclusion by attending to all students' learning needs, particularly for students who are at risk of underachievement.
- Promote student and teacher recognition

Impact on Teachers

1. Teachers will share and discuss learning outcomes, intentions, or objectives and success criteria with students more effectively and systematically.
2. Teachers will promote more quality discussion and interaction in the classroom using a range of techniques and focus particularly on the type and quality of questions they ask and how they help.

3. Teachers will improve quality of the verbal and written feedback they give students and assist students in using feedback to improve learning.
4. Students become willing and able to take more responsibility for their own learning and use self- and peer-assessment techniques to help each other learn.
5. Teachers will be able to diagnose learning patterns in students.
6. Teachers will develop assessments that are shared across the grade level.
7. Teachers will use planning time effectively and efficiently.
8. Teachers will assist in building a culture of collaboration at the school.

Expected Outcomes for Potomac Public Charter School
Students will be willing and able to take more responsibility for their own learning and use self- and peer-assessment techniques to help one another learn. Students will achieve.

Recommendations

Confidential and Highly Sensitive
General Recommendations

1. Grow Potomac teachers to support the demographics of the school
2. Recruit locally
3. Create new teacher cohorts, summer boot camps, and expert sessions
4. Increase diversity
5. Implement professional development for administrators that occurs throughout the year, aligned with school goals
6. Overhaul the current evaluation cycle and system
7. Establish a monthly case-management review team to examine internal practices

8. Pre-enrollment training for parents, continue commitment day, Saturday sessions for parents
9. 360-degree evaluations
10. Implement best human-capital strategies as benchmarked from other schools or LEAs
11. Institute technology improvements
12. Focus on pre-K (culture and support), grade 4 (culture and academics), bus riders (discipline and parent involvement), grade 8 (transition to high school)

Plan of Work—First 100 Days

This abbreviated list of tasks has been compiled to help ensure a smooth and orderly opening of school.

Instructional Program Preparation

o   Recruit and hire an operations director with a well-articulated plan
o   Review all job descriptions
o   Determine leadership and administrators and update and orient leaders
o   Check textbook inventories, report cards, and interim reports
o   Grade reporting policy and procedures
o   Get staff and student handbooks ready for distribution
o   Have field-trip policy guidelines reviewed, discussed, and distributed
o   Formalize and standardize lesson-plan template
o   Let teachers have written plans for the first day or two weeks of school
o   Check location and use of teacher equipment, materials, computers, etc.
o   Research public-address system or create a signal system to improve communications
o   Establish a system for regular monitoring of instruction and analysis of student results

o   Determine testing and assessment responsibilities (prepare for NWEA)

o   Finalize schedules (determine creative arts and specials)

o   Communicate the system for regular monitoring of instruction and analysis of student results (data talks, development of individual student profiles, parent involvement, etc.)

o   Fine-tune procedures for instructional activities, field trips, educational speakers, or use of videos

o   Create clubs for middle school (Student Government Association of Council for eighth graders)

o   Upgrade procedures for selection and approval of instructional materials

o   Upgrade substitute-teacher protocol and review leave policy

o   Get emergency-substitute folders and substitute-teacher-utilization procedures prepared and ready

o   Develop PBIS program

o   Orientation for substitutes and bus drivers

o   Research middle school library options (classroom libraries)

o   Create a pre-K program for high impact: parent-training program, parent shadowing, home visits (teachers and counselor), and Saturday seminars for parents

o   Prepare tool kits—parents, teachers, staff members

o   Have July–August PD plan (determine themes and presenters and prepare materials and surveys)

o   Plan for yearlong professional development and calendar (How will PD be used in the classroom?)

o   Schedule for learning walks

o   Prepare testing and assessment procedures and cycles

o   Determine classroom look-fors (every class)

o   Review curriculum for each grade or pacing guides and monitoring tools

o   Support teachers as they set up their rooms (nonnegotiable checklist provided)

o   Establish school-improvement team (meeting schedule, procedures, policies, roles)

Internal and External Communications

o   Communicate how report cards will be reviewed
o   Welcome/start up
    • Send letters home to all students and parents prior to the first day; send letters to teachers and staff
    • Ensure student packets are ready to take home—picture permission, medicine form, discipline plan, PTA membership invitation, volunteer procedures, MOUs for code of acceptable behavior, etc.
    • Prepare opening-school packets for parents (calendar, parenting tools, etc.)
o   Ensure that bulletin boards, banners, etc. are current (Potomac)
o   Print and disseminate activity and school calendar for August to September
o   Update information on the school website
o   Have a directory—teachers and staff and their addresses and phone numbers
o   Have an organization chart—show roles and responsibilities (who-to-go-to chart)
o   Work with parent liaison to form PTA
o   Schedule school-improvement team meeting
o   Meet with staff and students during the first week of school to present Code of Acceptable Behavior and Discipline Handbook
o   Ready internal communication procedures
o   Get requirements for honor roll, attendance awards, and other special awards
o   Communicate PBIS program
o   Others

Operational Procedures

o   Hire operations director or manager
o   Meet with building representative(s) and conduct walk-throughs
o   Share standards and develop procedures (i.e., fundraising, teacher supplies, textbooks, technology dissemination, locker assignments, teacher and staff mailboxes)
o   Review grants—title I (other)
o   Flip offices
o   Secure building keys, alarm system, keys, etc.
o   Create uniform procedures, promote uniform policy
o   Ensure all rooms have enough desks, chairs, tables
o   Convert multipurpose room to cafeteria-style format
o   Coordinate and have ready class lists, lunch schedules, bus assignments, arrivals, departures
o   Substitute food-service programs
o   Have a truancy plan
o   Paint and do general building repairs (possible parent paint party)
o   Have attendance-monitoring protocol, working with counselors
o   Review policy and procedure for security investigations, reporting harassment and discrimination, reporting child abuse, legal requirements for IDEA or 504
o   Have drills—fire or disaster
o   Clean
o   Clocks

Safety/Emergency Procedures

o   Procedure for fire drills and other emergencies
o   Signage: exit and entrance signs, fire-alarm covers, no-smoking directives posted in classrooms and cafeteria, etc.
o   Sign-in procedure
o   Safety committee established

- o   Monitoring cycle
- o   Facility-compliance manual
- o   Safety-procedure manual
- o   Anti-bullying procedures
- o   Visitor procedures, badges, etc.
- o   Transportation procedures including violations

Student Orientation/Responsibilities

- o   Lesson-plan procedures
- o   Professional development
- o   Observation cycle and evaluations
- o   Procedures for courageous conversations and coaching
- o   Dress code
- o   Procedures for staff needing to leave school during the school day
- o   Attendance and punctuality
- o   Clubs and sponsorships
- o   Use of technology (Facebook)
- o   Others

Student Services

- o   The office staff is prepared for students and parents.
- o   Procedures are followed for enrolling students.
- o   Student insurance information is ready.
- o   Classroom and homeroom attendance rolls are ready.
- o   Tardy policy is posted.
- o   Attendance procedures are regulated.
- o   Attendance callback system for verification of student absences has been established.
- o   Testing schedule has been communicated.
- o   Volunteer help has been contacted.
- o   Procedures for handling students who have not met health requirements within specific timelines have been communicated.

- o A health program and sick-room procedures are ready (procedures for dispensing meds, classroom-emergency kits, training schedule for teachers).
- o Student accident forms and incident forms are ready.
- o Others

My findings were heartbreaking but empowering and beautiful.

I remember something from my work in charter school—"start with the end in mind." I knew what I wanted to accomplish in two years. I remembered the what-ifs and the mistakes of the past. But I knew that God is always working in our lives, willing to forgive and put a new song in our hearts.

It was time to display my passion; learn how to balance many things with the help of those delegation skills; be data-dependent daily; calculate our valuation monthly; and remember that school climate mirrors its culture.

I remembered that performance declines are normal but must be addressed. In fact, if the data dips, "get back to work!" Cautious optimism is important. Don't celebrate too soon.

The teachers that we hired were amazing people. But I wanted them to "bring more to the table." As the leadership team created the school calendar, we built in brain breaks and professional development days. We had sessions on the following:

1. mindfulness
2. *grit*
3. turnaround plan

Potomac Prep PCS Staff, Students, Parents Await News of School's Future Charter School Board Will Vote on Proposed Charter Revocation on February 10

Washington, DC (Web), February 09, 2016

In June 2014, Potomac Prep's board hired Dr. Marian White-Hood, the former chief academic officer for the Maya Angelou Public Charter Schools in the district and a former award-winning principal in Prince George's County.

Under White-Hood's leadership, test scores increased while truancy and suspensions dropped precipitously. She replaced lackadaisical and nonperforming teachers with instructors recognized for their skill and commitment in working with children. After-school tutoring and Saturday school were implemented. She held programs to bring parents into the school, such as the Principal's Parent Advisory, Saturday School STARS, and parent-training sessions. Extracurricular programs such as Student Government Association, an arts and culture club, athletics, cheerleading and a technology club were created.

Though test scores improved by double-digits, DCPCSB had set a deadline of one year for NWEA scores to increase by 70 percent. When Potomac Prep did not meet that standard, DCPCSB began efforts to close the school. Potomac Prep's board chair was notified the day before Thanksgiving that the board was moving to revoke the charter. School officials notified them that rules of the charter required that a public hearing had to be held to give them a chance to respond. One such hearing was held in December. A second hearing was held on January 14. Hundreds of supporters of the school attended. Parents talked about their children's progress. Teachers talked about successes. Members of the community talked about the success they have witnessed.

It seemed for many in attendance like déjà vu. A similar round of hearings in 2014 resulted in the school getting a year to improve its scores. However, that deadline was applied to tests given only four months later. White-Hood said she and the teachers simply did not have enough time in that short period to meet the 70 percent target set by DCPCSB. She stated, "Turnaround schools need two to three years and strong support from parents. Potomac Prep's students were a few points shy of meeting the required target. But the paradigm has shifted…parents are engaged; students want to learn; and they are also proud of their school and their personal accomplishments. We are of proud of this change and celebrate our students and parents."

Potomac Prep supporters said that during the January 14 hearing, some members of the DCPCSB were texting and appeared not to be paying attention to the speakers. Potomac Prep's attorney has asked for copies of the texts, saying school officials should have access to any communication between board members and their staff during the hearing on whether they would revoke the charter.

White-Hood said she and her staff have asked for additional time to continue the progress the students have made. She said she expects test scores to go up again this spring. Her staff would have had two years to work with the students.

Report from DCPCSB
Potomac's Request to Meet with the Board
Website

There has been a lot of concern about the proposed revocation of Potomac Preparatory Public Charter School (Potomac Prep). Our mission is to ensure students and families have access to a quality public charter school education. DC PCSB does this by, among other things, holding schools accountable to tough academic standards.

On December 14, 2015, DC PCSB voted to initiate revocation of Potomac Prep's charter because the school failed to meet the academic targets outlined in its Charter Amendment. This action was taken pursuant to the School Reform Act, which authorizes DC PCSB to revoke a school's charter if the school "has failed to meet the goals and student academic achievement expectations set forth in the charter."

It's important to remember that the vote to initiate revocation begins an administrative process. The board has not decided to close the school.

History of Potomac Prep

- November 2014: Potomac Prep PCS underwent a ten-year review. The school did not meet seventeen of its twenty goals and academic achievement expectations outlined in its charter.
- November 2014: Board initiated charter revocation against Potomac Prep PCS.
- December 2014: Board voted not to revoke the school's charter and instead approved the school's turnaround plan to continue to operate conditioned on the school meeting the amended charter targets in the 2014–2015 school year and beyond.

Specifically regarding the 2014–2015 school year, the amendment required Potomac Prep PCS to meet all of the following targets or relinquish its charter at the end of the 2014–2015 school year:

Amended Charter Targets

1. Target: The school will be within at least be 1 percentage point of or exceed the in-seat attendance rate for the charter sector for each of the three grade-level bands for school year 2014–2015.
    Result: Not met. Potomac Prep came within 1 percentage point of their target for prekindergarten through second grade but missed their target in grades 3–8 by 1.8 percent, therefore falling short of the overall target.
2. Target: 70 percent of all grade 3–8 students will score at or above the 40th percentile of NWEA-MAP national average or meet or exceed their spring typical growth target in math and reading.
    Result: Not met.
3. Target: The school will be at least within 0.1 point of the 2015 DC charter average in each of the three *class* domains.
    Result: Not met. While the school achieved the target in classroom organization, Potomac Prep failed to achieve this target in the areas of emotional and instructional support.
4. Target: 50 percent of kindergarten through second-grade students will meet or exceed typical growth in reading and math on the NWEA-MAP assessment.
    Result: Not met. Potomac Prep only collected NWEA-MAP growth data for first- and second-grade students—56.8 percent met the targets in reading but only 46.7 percent met their target in math.

5. Target: 75 percent of prekindergarten to grade 3 and prekindergarten to grade 4 students will meet or exceed their average growth goals on their every-child-ready assessment.
    Result: Met.

What This Means

Because Potomac Prep did not meet all the agreed-upon targets on December 14, 2015, the board voted to initiate charter revocation. Potomac Prep has requested an informal hearing that will take place on January 14, 2016, at the school beginning at 6:00 p.m.

Interested parties can submit public comment, attend in person, follow the conversation on Twitter or watch the webcast.

This is an opportunity for DC PCSB to listen to students, families, and community stakeholders about Potomac Prep and ask questions for clarification where necessary. Following the informal hearing, DC PCSB will vote on the proposed revocation at its meeting on January 25. Charter revocation is never a decision DC PCSB takes lightly, and we encourage public input.

Rebuilding a School—Potomac Prep

We rebranded the school, moved classrooms around, hired caring and competent teachers, created a testing and assessment plan that included the used of data throughout the year to drive instruction, and painted the entire building so it really look and felt different. There were inspirational banners, murals, and showcases or bulletin boards that seemed to come alive each day.

Operations, human resources, community involvement, grant-writing, and instruction were burning issues for me. Thus, the role of principal spiraled into head of school and consisted of the following tasks:

- Communicate with parents
- Manage staff

- Recruit and train staff
- Work with staff on performance issues and developmental goals
- Manage physical condition of the building and manage resources and budget
- Manage all required documents for staff and students
- Ensure facility meets all state and local requirements
- Ensure the center compliant with all federal and state laws
- Respond and follow up on all enrollment inquiries
- Give tours to prospective parents
- Plan activities such as staff meetings, meet and greet, open house, etc.

Since the facility was small and organized as a pre-K to grade-8 school, additional tasks were important to school success. They included the following:

- Provide resources and college information as early as elementary school
- Ensure a culturally relevant curriculum
- Review disciplinary policies for fairness, restorative practices
- Pre-K parent participation
- Data collection and using it appropriately
- Disaggregate by race and gender
- Mentoring and tutoring and homework assistance
- Focus groups—pre-K, elementary, and middle school
- Clubs (attendance, competition, out-of-school-time activities, winter and spring-break camps, summer programs)
- Violence-free and respectful climate
- Professional development including how to communicate with parents, students, and the community—"The tongue can be fire."

Classroom accommodations include

➤ graphic organizers
➤ sentence games and sentence starters
➤ summarizing
➤ assessment
➤ use of data
➤ color coding
➤ manipulatives
➤ modify content
➤ provide supports
➤ close proximity
➤ anchor charts
➤ peer scribing
➤ visual clues
➤ technology and head phones
➤ provide resources
➤ IEP process
  o referral
  o evaluation
  o determining eligibility
  o writing the IEP
  o IEP meeting
  o alternative assignments and assessments
  o learning goals
  o visual schedules
  o time
  o level of support
  o sensory items (fidgets)

Modifications

• quantity
• monitoring

From PCSPBC Website

Monday, January 11, 2016, 11:43 a.m.

Thanks for your leadership, Dr. White-Hood! It is my sincere hope that Potomac Preparatory Public Charter School retains its charter, and also that the District of Columbia Public Charter School Board projects what advocacy REALLY looks like, and that it supports schools achieving measurable growth as a part of ongoing, long-term efforts to turnaround performance.

Example of a Testimony by a Stakeholder

Thursday, January 14, 2016, 12:31 p.m.

I am truly saddened behind the decision to begin the process of revocation for Potomac Preparatory Public Charter School. I had the opportunity to work with both Lighthouse and Potomac Prep, and because of this, I have a different set of lenses based on my tenure here at Potomac. In this letter, I plan to bring your attention to the changes to the poor performance of our previous management company Lighthouse and the substantial strides that have been taken for the 2014–2015 school year. I was employed by Lighthouse in 2012. Immediately I noticed the poor instruction, negative school climate, and the need for improvement. Once the school received its ten-year review, I received confirmation on what I suspected about the school. Immediately following the review, we had the opportunity to obtain a new leader, Dr. White-Hood. This was an effort to turn the school around. Since Dr. White-Hood was elected principal, the school has made tremendous changes to clean up the mess that was left by the previous management company. Upon her arrival, the school was without curriculum, highly-qualified teachers, facility needs, and resources, to name a few. Without these key components, it makes it difficult for our scholars to succeed. Principal White-Hood created a turnaround plan to address the needs right away. This plan was strategic and followed with fidelity from Potomac Prep staff during the 2014–2015 school year. I am aware that the school was placed under yearly conditions after the ten-year review of the school. While the goals set forward by the board seemed reachable, there are many variables that were not taken into consideration. It is no secret that our scholars where missing out on a lot of instruction, and as a result, student's academic performance was low. After ten years of poor instruction, there is no way that it will only take one year to get students back on track, especially considering that students were many grade levels behind. It is important to note that our students have made a lot of growth in a small amount of time. In closing, I am writing this letter in hopes that you would reconsider your decision to begin the process of revocation. Our school has made great strides toward increasing the quality of instruction, school climate, and rigor in education. Students do not deserve to have their education interrupted because they barely missed goals that was set in comparison to state averages. This was not fair considering that the fact that the students where already behind. I urge you to capitalize on the growth that was made to uplift the students to do better.

Lessons Learned

1. Fidelity matters!
2. High-quality implementation is critical
3. No rubber-stamping!
4. Love is a guiding principle.

First Semester
Summary of Walk-Abouts and Teacher Observations

- ✓ The needs of every child are met through extra support and enrichment.
- ✓ Students were doing most of the heavy lifting.
- ✓ There was less teacher talk and more student work.
- ✓ Teachers were activating students' prior knowledge.
- ✓ They use activities and student work that engage students as active learners.
- ✓ Differentiation was happening in every class.
- ✓ Teachers used pacing and creative use of time.
- ✓ Teacher-to-student and student-to-student interactions were evident.
- ✓ There was appropriate accommodations for special-needs students.

- ✓ There were classroom rules and procedures that minimize downtime, promoted student discipline, and maximized student engagement.
- ✓ Reinforcement of student-wide normal was evident.
- ✓ Students' perseverance and persistence was noted in every class.

Basically, the new charter school boosted learning for *all* students.

Final Pages of the Potomac Story

When the school was closed by the DC Charter School Board, I was exhausted and hurt, yet relieved. I knew that I would complete all required documents for the closure.

Our attendance was approaching the mid-1990s; reading score targets were met; mathematics targets were nearly met; the budget was strong; and all the teachers were in attendance on the last day of school. Our turnaround plan was available for other schools to use. All goals, objectives, targets, and data were codified for those who would be brave enough to travel this road.

The administrators sponsored a farewell luncheon for all stakeholders. We celebrated with food, music, dancing, games, and testimonies.

Commentary

CHAPTER 8

Early Learning…Later Years

*I felt like I was breathing fresher, cleaner
air. There was a path forward?*

After Potomac closed, I took a four-month vacation. I thought about my travels, the mountains I climbed, and the rocky roads that I hiked. I thought about the highs and the lows…the thunder and storms. But something haunted me. I felt incomplete. I had so many questions about the journey. Why the mountains, the rocky roads? Why the thunder and storms? I realized that there were so many things that I did not know—and as usual, I did not know what I did not know.

I realized that I needed to examine the beginnings…early learning, preschool, childcare. Just what practices impact the toddler? How do three-year-olds navigate the world of language? When do children begin to differentiate people, race, age, gender? What do preschoolers bring to kindergarten?

I found myself interviewing for a different position—senior childcare director for early learning and school-age programs.

Nonprofit Childcare Facility

I joined the team in November 2017 before COVID-19. I was definitely overqualified for the position, but I wanted to rekindle my journey in education. I wanted to begin at the beginning, tackling these questions:

1. What do childcare program offer parents?
2. What is the difference between early learning and childcare programs? Or are they one and the same?
3. What is the transition from pre-K to kindergarten?
4. How do pre-K children perform in kindergarten?
5. Why are young children suspended in elementary school?
6. And the list goes on and on...

So I joined the center as senior director, responsible for two programs: school-age and childcare center.

The *school-age program* struggled because it used an archaic framework; it was not competitive with other programs in the area. We served approximately sixty children who attended ten elementary school. Children arrived at 7:00 a.m. and were picked up by school buses at 8:30 a.m. The children attended one of the ten schools, boarded the bus at the end of the day, and were transported to the after-care program, where they participated in activities, had a snack, and were supervised by teacher assistants until 6:30 p.m. (pickup time). There was a school-age director who supervised approximately seven staff members. This program was licensed but not accredited.

The *childcare-center program* began at 7:00 a.m. and ended at 6:30 p.m. This program was housed in the main childcare building. There were nine classrooms and eighteen to twenty-four teachers and one director in the center. The center enrolled children eighteen months to five years old. Most of the time, we were in ratio; however, there were some troubling areas. This program was licensed but not accredited.

Leadership Challenges

1. The center needed a playground.
2. The teachers needed to obtain their credentials; I put the teachers in three tiers to create professional plans for growth.
3. The center needed a business manager.

4. The director was not certified for the position, did not have an AA degree.
5. Many times, we were short-staffed, with high turnover because of wages.
6. Food functions were less than perfect.
7. The teachers rarely received recognition or rewords; I created a teacher-of-the-month program.

It was clear that the company was in denial. It did not know the demographics of the community, the staff, or the parents. A feasibility plan for expansion did not exist. An improvement plan did not exist. The only data that was available related to finances and tuition. I would call it "data insecurity." The company did not know what it did not know. It did not use demographic, employment, or health reports.

My Job Description Summary

Directs, organizes, and administers childcare programs.

General Accountabilities

➤ Directs integrated programs covering basic child care, education, social service, nutrition, and parent involvement and education.

➤ Supervises the development and coordination of curriculum, activities, and special programs for children.

➤ Develops and manages childcare-program budgets.

➤ Ensures program operations are compliant with donor, grant, or regulatory agencies requirements.

➤ Liaises with parent groups and coordinates the implementation of support services and activities.

➤ Implements suggestions received from parents as appropriate.

> ➤ Ensures adherence to established admissions guidelines.
> ➤ Ensures adequate records and files are maintained for each child.
> ➤ Generates reports as required based on program activity.
> ➤ Directs the maintenance of the childcare facility, parking area, play yards, and outside equipment.

The company reserves the right to add or change duties at any time.

Job Qualifications

1. Education: bachelor's degree
2. Experience: 5–7 years of related experience

Skills

1. excellent verbal and written communication
2. problem-solving skill
3. active listening
4. monitoring
5. instructing
6. leadership
7. coordination
8. social perceptiveness
9. judgment and decision-making
10. learning strategies

I thought about the importance of living a godly life. I met with the executive director and associate executive director many times to share my vision for the two programs. I was able to speak to power. In fact, I fought the upper leadership to accept my voice…to hear my voice.

As stated in the Center of Excellence for Infant and Early Childhood Mental Health Consultation (SAMHSA, n.d.):

> Worthy compensations is paramount in an equitable workplace, but it is not the only consideration. Other equity factors to consider are

- Diversity and inclusion,
- Opportunities for professional growth,
- Professional recognition that reflects the importance of the work, and
- Factors such as fair distribution of work, time, and responsibility.

> A fundamental requirement of any profession is that the people working within it view themselves as professionals and share a professional identity that includes commonly held values and ways of thinking about their work and the world. (Mead 2019)

What I Remember Most

- fresh vision and passion
- tier teachers
- reigniting the passion
- my redeemer lives

Note from a Professional Developer

Dr. White-Hood,

I just enjoy working with you. You are a true professional who believes in providing their staff with professional development and advancement. Unfortunately, in our field, we lack owners, administrators, and directors who are not willing to provide or work with their staff or employees in their professional development. I truly hope and pray your staff greatly appreciate your education to them and to this field.

Dr. ——

Lessons Learned

➤ Parents want to know that their children's teachers are qualified.
➤ Parents want to be a part of the school (monthly breakfasts).
➤ The importance of early learning—indelible ink—cannot be erased.

Commentary

CHAPTER 9

The Antagonist—the COVID-19 Pandemic of 2020

Chapter 9 was supposed to be about the next road in my leadership journey. But *chapter 9* is about the antagonist called COVID-19 and adjusting to its variables omicron and ——? A seemingly never-ended battle!

Because of the ups and downs, surges, vaccines, and boosters, masks and masks off, no airplane flights, and changes from one state to another…one country to another, COVID-19 has created a *dark* place on this planet and in my life as an educator. It has had a destabilizing effect on me!

I am avoiding crowds and sanitizing my hands so much that I may not have fingerprints anymore. This *dark* season was long and challenging. It created a crisis in the field of education. For example, in education, there were numerous program shutdowns. In addition, (1) teachers were leaving the profession—retiring; (2) child-care workers quit their jobs; (3) socially distancing oneself from children was heartbreaking and stressful; (4) colleges and university programs in education closed; (5) careers in education were frozen; and (6) relationships loss their importance.

But I know that Christ will hold me steadfast! A *symbol of hope* is found in every breath I take, in every child I come in contact with, and in every book in the Bible.

We have to get ready for the new things in life. I know that God has something in store for the profession—*job* in the Bible.

And I decide to document my journey…write the book that my mom asked me to write before she passed on!

Lessons Learned

1. Don't let the dark seasons keep you down.
2. Discover talents that I did not know I had.

<table>
<tr><td>

Commentary

</td></tr>
</table>

CHAPTER 10

Early Learning: What It Is and What It Could Be

A Private Licensed Day-Care Experience

I joined the team of ——— in November 2021 during the pandemic. I was drawn to the school by several factors: (1) having a different experience—Reggio, (2) yearning to work with teachers, (3) wanting to expand my knowledge base, and (4) wanting to use my experience to grow the center while focusing on accreditation.

My first weeks were complicated, or should I say, confusing because there was no real orientation to VA, the school, the teachers. I had to learn how to navigate the ——— landscape. A senior director visited the school to train me how to tackle the outdated payroll and tuition system. The woman who hired me was the owner.

Troubled Waters

- Seven of the eight teachers have been at the school for more than fifteen years.
- There was no pension system.
- Some teachers complained of bias and inequality.
- There was no research-based management or operation system.

Soon, I learned a new word—*hubris*. She was exhibiting hubris or arrogance—the owner didn't seem to value humility, her teachers, and the concept of early learning. Immediately, my voice was muted! The owner made judgments about teachers and used abusive speech.

I believed that exclusionary rather than inclusionary practices were being applied brutally to my being. I felt implicit bias and classism because of the subtle comments, actions, and words that hurt! I was stuck! I knew that I could leave, but there was something keeping me there. I wore the director's shoes, but they felt tight and uncomfortable.

I needed to practice "job-crafting." What could I do to change my role as director in this school? How could I make the role more engaging and satisfying (Berg, Wrzesniewski, and Dutton 2008)?

The childcare assignment was a low point in my life. I felt pinned in, could not go up or down, forward or backward. I felt as though I was in shallow water. The radio ministry helped a bit, but I yearned for the pre-pandemic interaction. The kind of interaction that touched my soul, singing songs, kneeling at the altar, and embracing others.

I had an allergic reaction to the practice of the school owner. For her, it was about money, money, money instead of the quality of the program. Her communication style is traumatizing, bullying, and belittling. Her unwholesome words tear down instead of build up a person. This childcare experience was the lowest point in my career (life). I felt as though I were a prisoner in my own skin. I was having an allergic reaction to *her* selfish practices. The phone calls from the owner steals my peace and joy. Her love of money trumps high quality—unthinkable! Wildly untenable! I was losing my edge, my passion, my spirit.

Just think: kindness is contagious! A little kindness from the *top* would mean so much to the teachers and filter down to the children. I yearned for the peace of God.

My greatest fear—that this negative experience would impact the wealth of experience that I enjoyed previously. The enemy was trying to stop me from where I was going. How could I push back? Rise up?

I was not learning, growing, and becoming a better leader. In fact, I believed that there was a *disinformation campaign* in progress!

During the time that I was in the school, I realized that aggression leads to mistrust, poor health, and stress that is toxic. I learned that there were growing concerns from at least four of the eight teachers.

Despite the serious challenges, I read scriptures in the morning and evening for a renewed sense of purpose. The Lord's blessings are abundant and fruitful. In this private school, I learned these:

- Give people time to endear change
- Enjoy pre-K teachers and the drama of schooling
- Recognize difficulties (i.e., licensing, credentialing, training)
- Be willing to forgive self and others
- Acknowledge the worst lies are the ones you tell yourself
- Realize it's never too late to lay a sturdy foundation
- Turn the negativity into a positive
- Dispel the myth of old age
- Stay positive in a toxic setting
- Emotions control us – but we can control them

I believe that God's plan for me was to think differently, act differently.

1. Mirror man
2. Reread my dissertation
3. Go through my library and read dog-eared pages
4. Check in (literature) do the research
5. Talk to someone you trust
6. Reclaim the philosophy of education that I have lived by for years
7. Turn my thoughts into action
8. Codify—what can others do
9. Be willing to see what's possible

Like Paul, confidence energizes us; drives out any worry, fear, or doubt; leaves us with workable assurance. As Philippians 4:10–13 reminds, I believe that "I can do all things through Christ who strengthens me." I'm putting my trust in God, talking to *him*, drawing close to *him* in prayer. So I will face each day, victoriously in spite of what is seen.

Someone once said, "If you play with dirt, it will rub off on you." So I decided to leave this school after one year. I did not want the owner's philosophy and practices to rub off on me. I believed them to be inherently *wrong*.

I did not have another position, but I believed that "Christ is *all*—he is my everything." Decades of my life in education transformed me from a young teen to a seventy-plus woman. God directed my path and generously gave me a special gift. I definitely needed to hit the Refresh button and move on. I reflected on the experience at the private childcare center, then asked myself one question: How would I change my focus in life? I know that whatever you ask God for, it's already done.

I thought about the book I started and realized that the final chapters were ready to be typed and printed. These final chapters will bring joy and wonder to my heart, incredible peace and comfort to my soul.

Lessons Learned

- Don't put someone down just to elevate yourself.
- *Bitter cold!* I yearned for my pre-pandemic life!
- The evil eye is unloving.
- Develop the art of silence.
- Fill your mind with positive thoughts.

Commentary

97

CHAPTER 11

The Present
Yearning For and Needing More

Misty-colored memories. The way we were.

What's my truth?

Nearing the end of my journey causes me to reflect. I think about the good times and the bad. I recall the times that I gave my teachers a slow yes instead of a fast no. And the *yes* felt great. I also think about the years that I operated in the spirit of humility, serving God instead of myself.

I think about the errors that I have made—times I fumbled the ball, slipups, miscalculations, and poor choices. I think about the words that I wish I could take back—my anger when a poor teacher hurt a child. Sometimes, I would start at 1 and ramp up to 150, unapologetically! God's mercy is bigger than my mistakes.

I cannot count the number of times God has saved me, but I can remember many things—memories flashed through my mind… memories of walking through the storms of life.

You can't be a slacker and an authentic educator in the same space. In fact, we don't do what we do because it's easy, but because it's right. I realize that God called me to the field of education…to use it for his glory.

I cherish the memories of God's grace…how *he* provided me with exactly what I needed, when I needed it. Often, *he* gave me parental responsivity—warmth, nurturance, consistency. No one is beyond the reach of God. Sometimes, *he* gave me a deep appreciation for family and friends. Thank you, thank you, thank you, God.

What I now know, the people that I have met, the books I have read, the experiences that have become part of my being, the skills that I have gained have been transformative. I ask myself, "Have I reached my ultimate goal?"

The journey has been a relentless process of *becoming*. I believe that I still have a path to follow. My relationship with God tells me so—that relationship makes all the difference. Because of our relationship, I know that "He leads me; He restores me; He makes me lie down in green pastures; He is with me," (Psalm 23).

Impartial Conclusion

I am still walking my journey after decades in education. I am grateful that I discovered my gift early in life, cultivated it, and used it for the grace of God. I am honored that you have read my story. It's not the end.

Lesson Learned

Sometimes we don't know we can do something until we do it.

Commentary

CHAPTER 12

Conclusion
A Journey Remembered!

*I've learned that making a living is not
the same thing as making a life.*

—Maya Angelou

This journey has given me love and joy on an unimaginable scale. And there is no way to really explain the transformative impact that the Bible has had on my life. I have experienced failures, mistakes, and falls, but God helped me get up, brush myself off, and start walking down the road again. *He* feeds the hunger in my heart.

Honestly, I love what my life has been, my leadership has been… helping teachers, helping students, helping parents and families, and being a huge part of something larger than myself. The words resonate: "To much is given, much is expected!"

In retrospect, I continue to build on the lessons that I have learned. One lesson is that the devil will set his sights on the leader—the quarterback in football, for example. In war times, the enemy goes after the leader!

Another lesson is that, the leader must be proactive and vigilant. Don't get sidetracked! Stay focused and be willing to grow and learn. The leader must THINK:

Be *truthful.*
Be *helpful.*
Be *inspiring.*
Be *necessary.*
Be *kind.*

The leader must not be afraid to speak truth to power. Speaking truth takes many forms—sharing research findings; actively participating in professional associations; conducting trainings and workshops; writing articles; providing testimony at board meetings; and serving on national, state, and local committees.

There is no doubt about it. My early beginnings set me on a unique path to create a profound cultural shift…to be in "everyone's home" each evening. With God, I had to power through! *He* gives us wisdom. His unconditional love protects us, and we need not fear or be anxious for anything (Philippians 4:4–7).

We are infused with the power to help and be a resource to others. We are infused with the power to show grace and to connect with others. I recount Lois A. Cheney's words, "You find you are made up of bits and pieces of all who have touched your life, and you are more because of it."

I *thank all* of you who have been a part of my life. You put smiles in my heart. *Thank you* for holding my hand! *Thank you* for feeding my passion. I truly appreciate the confidence you showed in me. I can't wait to see how my life story will end.

I plunged deeply into what is comfortable to me—the special fall issue of *Phenomenology & Practice*, volume 6, no. 2 (2012): 1–7. I, still respect the pedagogical direction laid out by the great philosophers.

I continue to believe that children want to learn, to grow, to be recognized, to be loved and nurtured. And we must do all we can to *help and support* them. Just what does that look like? What does the *help and support* look like? We know *why* but *how*? When? And what does it mean to help and support?

God has ordained my steps. I'm still trying to fulfill God's purpose for my life. The work gives me a reason for living. I am here for such a time as this. You *cannot* lose, by giving yourself to God.

As stated by Amanda Gorman, Poet Laureate and activist (2021), in "The Hill We Climb" at Joe Biden's inauguration as US president on January 2021, "For there is always light, if only we're brave enough to see it. If only we're brave enough to be it." Gorman's inaugural poem captured viewers across the country and made her an overnight literary sensation. At her young age, she inspires me… she is my *shero*!

There is more work to be done…

- Critical-race theory
- Racism, classism, and other "isms"
- Replacement theory
- Poverty
- Black Lives Matter
- All Lives Matter
- Crisis at the border
- The insurrection and spread of disinformation
- Crime on the rise
- Concentric circle of trauma
- Defenseless children are hostages of gun violence—school shootings like those in Sandy Hook, San Bernardino, Columbine, and Robb Elementary School in Texas.
- Food insecurity
- Homelessness
- Crisis in the classroom including teacher shortages

And all the other theories that turn man against man, boy against boy. We must make sure that outstanding educators don't abandon their calling! I believe that the Lord wants us to carry the anointing to others in schools, communities, and the world. (Isaiah 60)

I believed that I am blessed. I am valuable. I am confident. I am healthy. I am creative. I am working my way to heaven. I can reach my destiny. I can be the best self that I could be…with God! I am forgiven, and I am restored. I am surrounded by excellence—the children, teachers, and parents. I am equipped. It's in me! I can do anything through Christ! "Take pride in how far you've come. Have faith in how far you can go. But don't forget to enjoy the journey," says Michael Josephson, in the matchless name of Jesus.

I know that God is still working in me. He is a God of justice. I never forget the *God factor*! It's where leadership comes from—the God factor! God is in the restoration business. He has supernatural properties.

Now has anyone else thought of just returning to the biblical model for answers? Just what is another way this book might end? Would you recommend this book to a friend? Why? Why not?

Commentary

REFERENCES

Berg, Justin M., Amy Wrzesniewski, and Jane E. Dutton. 2008. "What Is Job Crafting and Why Does It Matter?" Center for Positive Organizational Scholarship. Michigan Ross School of Business.

Heifetz, R. A., and M. L. Linsky. 2002. *Leadership on the Line: Staying Alive through the Dangers of Leading.* Boston, Massachusetts: Harvard Business School Press.

Schlechty, P. C. 2009. *Leading for Learning: How to Transform Schools Into Learning Organizations.* San Francisco, California: Jossey-Bass.

"The Opportunity Atlas: Mapping the Childhood Roots of Social Mobility." CES-18–42 (September 2018).

The Social World of Children: Learning to Talk.

ABOUT THE AUTHOR

With over forty years of committed service to education, Dr. White-Hood has been an advocate for intense and rigorous levels of curriculum and instruction that includes programs that address the needs of *all* children. She has embraced parents as partners in public-school education and has modeled the intent of parent involvement in education from the federal law.

In addition, she has used proven research-based methods, strategies, and practices to give tremendous energy and focus to pre-IN through high school practices. Winner of the Prince George's County Chamber of Commerce Outstanding Educator Award, Prince George's County Public Schools Outstanding Educator Award, finalist in the Maryland Teacher of the Year Competition, *Washington Post* Distinguished Leadership Award, and 2002 Minority Achievement Award, Dr. White-Hood never gives up on children, parents, or community members!

Dr. Marian White-Hood has trained, mentored, and coached over thirty teachers who have become principals and administrators in the metropolitan area. Likewise, she has trained principals for the Department of Defense in Germany.

In closing, Dr. White-Hood has been creative and innovative in academically, socially, and emotionally educating youth. Today, Dr. Marian White-Hood is honored to be the director for an early-learning program in Maryland, training and supervising teachers and spreading her love of and appreciation for children. In her spare time, she plans educational programs, supports a ministry for homeless males in the Washington, DC, area, and continues to write about her journey as a leader.